ASIAN CAPITALISTS IN THE EUROPEAN MIRROR

COMPARATIVE ASIAN STUDIES

General editor: Dick Kooiman
Assistant editor: Karin Peperkamp, Centre for Asian Studies Amsterdam

Publications in this series:

CENTRE FOR ASIAN STUDIES AMSTERDAM

Mario Rutten

Asian Capitalists in the European Mirror

VU University Press
Amsterdam, 1994

VU University Press is an imprint of:
VU Boekhandel/Uitgeverij bv
De Boelelaan 1105
1081 HV Amsterdam
The Netherlands

Editing by: A. Stronge, Amsterdam
Layout by: Avo-text, Amstelveen
Printed by: Ridderprint, Ridderkerk

ISBN   90-5383-270-X CIP
NUGI 653

Contents

1. Introduction

For the past two decades, studies on South and Southeast Asia have been emphasizing the emergence of a new class of capitalist entrepreneurs, consisting of rich farmers, traders and industrialists. Although most of these studies emphasize the socio-economic and socio-political importance of this new class of entrepreneurs, they usually point to the specific capitalist nature of their economic and social behaviour, and of the economy in which they operate. South Asian capitalists have been described as 'commercially oriented industrialists', 'merchant capitalists' and 'financier industrialists' who operate in an economy characterized as an 'intermediate form of capitalist development', a 'constrained type of merchant capitalism' and 'commercialism'. The terms 'rent capitalists', 'statist capitalists', 'comprador capitalists', 'hesitant capitalists', 'trader industrialists' and 'capitalist bureaucrats' have been employed to describe the capitalists in Southeast Asia while their economies have been characterized as 'rent capitalism', 'bureaucratic capitalism', 'statist capitalism', 'dependent capitalism' and 'ersatz capitalism'.

What all these characterizations have in common is disapproval of the behaviour of the present-day rich farmers, traders and industrialists in South and Southeast Asia. The specific capitalist nature of this class to which the studies on South and Southeast Asia refer, is considered to be a deformed, a pseudo- or non-genuine capitalist nature. Underlying this common view is the assumption that, either at present or in the past, either in Asia or in another part of the world, there did exist a class of pure, genuine and true capitalists. Without actually referring to the European path of industrial transition, it is this path and its emergence of a class of industrial capitalists that is frequently invoked as model or paradigm for the behaviour of the capitalists operating in South and Southeast Asia today. It is generally assumed that the early European industrialists, i.e. those entrepreneurs who operated in Europe at the time of the Industrial Revolution - mid-eighteenth to the mid/late-nineteenth century - did meet the characteristics of true and genuine capitalists that the present-day South and Southeast Asian entrepreneurs are said to be lacking.

1

Following the fact that any comparison of European history with contemporary developments in Asia is usually regarded as historical determinism, comparisons of the emergence of the South and Southeast Asian entrepreneurs with their European counterparts remain implicit. As a result, most references to the 'merchant', 'constrained' or 'rent' type of capitalist behaviour of the present-day South and Southeast Asian entrepreneurs are partly based on assumptions about the origins and nature of European industrialists of which the validity is seldom questioned. Viewing the persistency and value attached to these characterizations, it is important that these assumptions are made explicit and are tested on their tenability.

This essay deals with the capitalists in Asia and with the early industrialists in Europe.[1] It discusses the 'Asian capitalists in the European mirror'. This title, being derived from the series of lectures by Gerschenkron (1970), is broad and ambitious. Following Gerschenkron's opening statement I also want to emphasize that its actual subject matter is much more narrow and much more modest. Essentially, I should like to show what light, if any, is shed by the study of the early European industrialists on the selected issue of characterizing the capitalist class in contemporary South and Southeast Asia.

In the next section of the essay, I present an overview of the characterizations of the present-day capitalists in South and Southeast Asia. Following this overview, I argue in the third section that these characterizations are partly based on assumptions about the first industrialists in Europe. To what extent are these assumptions valid in the light of the findings of historical studies on the European industrialists? This issue is dealt with in the fourth section in which I discuss some historical studies on the emergence of the early industrialists in Europe. What light do these findings shed on the prevailing views on the emergence of the capitalist class in South and Southeast Asia? In the fifth and concluding section of the essay, I argue that, partly because scholars studying Asian society have seldom made use of new insights among the European economic historians to question their assumptions about the early industrialists in Europe, our view on the emergence of the capitalist class in South and Southeast Asia has been a distorted one.

2

2. Characterizing the Asian Capitalists

For a very long time already, developments in South and Southeast Asia have inspired scholars to invent a terminology specific to the region because they believed that the processes studied did not seem to fit into the existing type of classification. Marx's 'Asiatic mode of production', Furnivall's 'plural society' and Boeke's 'dual economy' are perhaps the most well-known concepts that were conceived in colonial times to analyse the South and Southeast Asian societies.[2] In the last two decades, several new concepts have been employed to analyse the present-day developments in South and Southeast Asia. The mode of production of the South Asian economy in general and that of India in particular has been characterized in terms of a 'semi-feudal mode of production' (Bhaduri 1973; Chandra 1974; Sau 1975), a 'semi-colonial semi-feudal mode of production' (Sen Gupta 1977) and a 'dual mode of production' (Lin 1980). Its economy has been described as a 'constrained type of merchant capitalism' (Harriss 1981), an 'intermediate form of capitalist development' (Harriss 1982) and a socio-economic structure dominated by 'commercialism' (Van der Veen 1976; Streefkerk 1985).[3] The terms 'rent capitalism' (Fegan 1981), 'bureaucratic capitalism' (Robison 1986), 'statist capitalism' (Jomo 1988), 'dependent capitalism' and 'ersatz capitalism' (Yoshihara 1988) have been employed to analyse the Southeast Asian economies, such as those of Indonesia, Malaysia and the Philippines.

What all these concepts have in common is the insistence that the characteristics of South and Southeast Asian developments are so specific that they merit a terminology specific to the region. The relations of production in these societies are held to be of a mixed nature. Capitalist and pre-capitalist relations of production are intertwined without any tendency of capitalist relations becoming more dominant. Merchant or financial capital is powerfully developed at the expense of productive capital; capital circulation instead of capital accumulation is the dominant tendency in South and Southeast Asia. Development of South and Southeast Asian capitalism has been largely confined to the tertiary sector: commerce, trade and services. The manufacturing sectors of the economy - agriculture and industry - have not been the driving force of economic growth in these countries. Development in South and Southeast Asia has not been the result of self-generating and self-sustaining autonomous economic growth, based on an open-market economy and fuelled by indigenous technology and serviced by indigenous skills. More than anything else, economic growth in South and Southeast Asia is considered to be a dependent type of development: dependent on foreign capital, foreign technology, distorted market mechanisms and a high level of government protection and state assistance.

One factor which is considered to be crucial in determining the nature of capitalist development in South and Southeast Asia has been the process by which the capitalist class emerges. Characterizations of the developments in South and Southeast Asia as a specific type of capitalism have therefore often been based on references to the characteristics of the capitalists operating in these countries. Developments in India have been characterized as merchant capitalist developments, Indian society as dominated by merchant capitalism, because the capitalists operating in India are commercially oriented capitalists or merchant capitalists (Harriss 1981; Harriss 1982; Van der Veen 1976; Streefkerk 1985). Developments in Indonesia are characterized as dependent capitalist or bureaucratic-capitalist developments, Indonesian society as dominated by dependent capitalism or bureaucratic capitalism, because the capitalists operating in Indonesia are dependent capitalists or bureaucratic capitalists (Robison 1986; Yoshihara 1988). Developments in Malaysia are characterized as statist-capitalist developments, Malaysian society as dominated by statist capitalism, because the capitalists operating in Malaysia are statist-capitalists (Jomo 1988). And to conclude this summing-up: developments in the Philippines are characterized as rent capitalist developments, Philippine society as dominated by rent capitalism, because the capitalists operating in the Philippines are rent capitalists (Fegan 1981).

South and Southeast Asian capitalists are a specific type of capitalists because they display a commercial orientation and follow a business strategy characterized by diversification of economic interests. In his study on Southeast Asia, Yoshihara Kunio employs the terms 'rent seekers' to emphasize that 'many business leaders have a short time-horizon and go after quick profits. A number of industrialists have diversified into real estate and non-manufacturing fields, instead of concentrating on technological improvement and slowly building up industrial empires' (Yoshihara 1988: 4). In his study on rural capitalism in the Philippines, Brian Fegan also emphasizes the specific type of economic diversification among the class of rural capitalists who do not directly apply capital to the production process in agriculture or industry itself but gain control of the claims on the product

4

of others through the outlay of merchant or financial capital. In order to characterize this specific behaviour of the rural upper class in the Philippines, Brian Fegan argues for a revival of the term 'rent capitalist' as coined by Bobek (1962). The rent-capitalist 'expands operations by using money to gain claims on the product of more petty units of production via mortgages, purchases, and loans. The rent capitalist reserves his capital for speculation in products and land and for making loans to petty producers for materials of production, instruments of production, for luxuries, for ceremonies, and for emergencies. All these give the rent-capitalist claims on the product of the petty producer' (Fegan 1981: 2). At the same time it leaves him free of involvement in the production process. This lack of connection between the capitalist and production means that the members of the capitalist class in the Philippines are essentially buy and sell merchants and moneylenders who set the rate of return as high as the market will bear, who do not apply fixed capital to the production process itself, who do not expend money at risk for instruments or materials for production or wages, and who do not exercise any kind of supervision over the work process (ibid.: 8-9).

In a study on commercialization and accumulation in a village in Central Java, Indonesia, Frans Hüsken also emphasizes the specific characteristics of large farmers who continue to make use of pre-capitalist types of relations - sharecropping, rentals of land and corvée labour - and who invest a large part of their agricultural surplus in non-productive types of activities such as trade, usury and speculation. While discussing this aspect of economic diversification and the nature of the farmers' involvement in the production process, Hüsken suggests the term 'hesitant capitalists', rather than 'rent capitalists', to explain for the fact that many large farmers do invest part of their surplus in agricultural production or in the processing of agricultural products, and are pushing their sharecroppers either directly or indirectly through their overseers to increase their yields as much as possible. 'To call them pure rent-capitalists in the Bobekian sense would therefore leave too many aspects of their behaviour unexplained. A better term would probably be that of 'hesitant capitalists' who in the face of their suddenly increased surplus and well aware of its fragility shrink at a too heavy involvement in capitalist investments'.[4]

Lack of connection between the capitalist and the production process is also emphasized by Braadbaart and Wolters in their study on industrial entrepreneurs in rural West Java. They employ the term 'trader industrialists' to indicate that leading entrepreneurs in rural industry in West Java are primarily trade-oriented with production coming only in second place. 'The business elites are engrossed in trade as much as in production, and have not ... tried to assume direct control over the manufacturing process. Rather, they direct available time and resources to the build-up of market outlets to which they then hitch the industry as it is, minimising their interference with the production aspect' (Braadbaart and Wolters 1992: 54). According to these authors, the consequence of this business strategy is that the production aspect holds a somewhat peripheral position in the activities of these rural industrial elites. Rather than producers, the leading industrial entrepreneurs in West Java are to be characterized as 'trader industrialists' (ibid.: 77).

The fact that capitalists do not involve themselves directly in the production process but operate through investments in trade, usury and speculation is also emphasized in various studies on South Asia, more in particular on India. In her study on traders in North Arcot district, Tamil Nadu, Barbara Harriss for example argues that although the dominant form of trade is capitalist, it is a 'constrained type of merchant capitalism' which prevails (Harriss 1981: 209). Profits are to a large extent obtained by appropriating surplus labour from indebted household producers; they are based on the existence of non-capitalist relations of production, such as debt relationships of wage labourers to the firm and ties of debt between traders and peasants (ibid.: 208). She shows that these profits are only very rarely invested in non-agricultural productive activity. 'Commerce, consumption and agricultural production are much more important destinations for accumulated capital' (ibid.: 94). According to John Harriss who studied the farming community in the same district, neither did a class of rural capitalists emerge in the agricultural sector of the economy. He shows how the class of substantial owner-cultivators does invest substantially in the superior means of agricultural production, appropriates surplus value and maintains a cycle of extended production based on accumulation. 'They might be described therefore as constituting a category of capitalist farmers. But in some instances the same people are also moneylender/merchants who exploit the large mass of dependent households through usury and through their control of the product of such households; and these activities may yield a better rate of return than reinvestments in production. ... The intensification of capital in agricultural production is therefore constrained by the development of merchant, moneylending capital' (Harriss 1982: 285). Instead of using the term 'capitalist farmers', he employs the term 'landlord-kulak-usurer-merchant combine'[5] to account for the fact that impressive parts of the surpluses generated by the substantial owner-cultivators of this district flow mainly into trade, and trading profits again flow back into the agrarian economy in the form of money-lending or commercial capital.

In her study on farmers-turned-businessmen in Andhra Pradesh, Carol Upadhya also argues that the pattern of diversification of business interests and assets tends to inhibit innovation and rapid growth because few entrepreneurs are willing to invest all they have in a single productive undertaking. The result is a flow of capital into numerous small businesses. 'Entrepreneurs prefer to invest in small service industries with guaranteed incomes and low capital outlays, such as transport, hotels, and contracting, rather than in capital-intensive manufacturing industries. ... Thus, it remains to be seen whether these farmers-turned-businessmen will emerge as a class of true industrial capitalists' (Upadhya 1988: 1439). In a similar line, Ranjit Sau stresses the constrained nature of the pattern of economic diversification among the Indian capitalists. According to him, 'Landlords and capitalist farmers who gather some amount of surplus for investment can at best aspire to set up a small company in industry. But thereafter their progress is blocked. The relatively modest and volatile rate of profit in a small company and the lack of avenues for further advancement may work as a barrier to the transition of landlords and capitalist farmers into the class of industrial capitalists' (Sau 1984: PE-75; see also Sau 1988: 794).

Several studies that focus on the class of industrialists in India also emphasize the specific pattern of economic diversification among the members of this class. In his study on small-scale industrial entrepreneurs in Gujarat, West India, Jan-Herre van der Veen stresses the fact that these entrepreneurs display a commercial orientation: they are interested in quick gain instead of long-term ventures, and they prefer financial flexibility to tying up a substantial portion of their capital in fixed assets. According to Van der Veen, the result is the emergence of a class of commercially oriented, instead of production-oriented industrial entrepreneurs. '(T)hese industrialists tend to expend considerable effort on the purchasing and marketing aspects of their firms and tend to expend negligible effort on the production aspects of their firms. Rather than applying their energies to reducing the costs of production, they apply their energies to reducing purchasing costs and enhancing sales receipts. It is usually presumed that these patterns of behaviour are inappropriate to industrial entrepreneurs. Industrial entrepreneurs must be concerned with all aspects of an enterprise: purchasing, production, marketing, and so on. But their primary concerns, especially in a country trying to industrialize rapidly, are *supposed* to be concerns related to production: utilization of full capacity, appropriate technology, labour productivity, and so on' (Van der Veen 1973: 47-8).

Along similar lines, Streefkerk stresses the inappropriateness of the commercial orientation of small-scale industrialists in the South Gujarat town of Bulsar. 'The results of the development of Bulsar's small industries ... are hardly encouraging ... because industrial entrepreneurship ... is characterized by commercialism, the tendency to set up, successively or simultaneously, diverse commercial and industrial activities' (Streefkerk 1985: 258). He suggests that this inclination of small-scale entrepreneurs to involve themselves, whether successively or simultaneously, in too wide a range of disparate commercial and industrial activities is typical of small-scale industrialists all over India.[6]

It is this type of commercially oriented industrialists that is termed 'financiers' or 'financier industrialists' by Mark Holmström. He contrasts these 'financiers' with the 'technicians' who differ from each other in background, attitudes, motivation and style of management. A financier 'thinks of the firm as a family investment, to be kept going for as long as it is more profitable than alternative investments. A technician may have access to family money, and he may take to the commercial side of the business, but his attitude to the firm is different: the product matters more to him, because his main assets are his knowledge of how to make it and his ideas about how to improve it or to use the experience to develop new products' (Holmström 1985: 88). According to Holmström, it is the technician who bears the closest resemblance to the old-style craftsman entrepreneur, who learned new skills by trial and error and improvisation, and who built up the business gradually by reinvesting profits. They are the ones who sometimes stress the moral independence of a self-made man who started with very little and made it by his own efforts. They are well known for their pride in their work, their delight in new technology and their stress on technical perfection (ibid.: 87, 100-2). 'The technician may be the real entrepreneur. ... Technicians are committed to a product and a technology not just by temperament and conditioning, but because it makes economic sense for them. ... If the failure rate is high, the successes benefit the national economy by raising production and employment, and by technical innovation. Financiers deliberately close firms down: the consequent reallocation of resources may benefit them but not the nation, and is disastrous for their workers' (ibid.: 106-7).

In sum, South and Southeast Asian capitalists are a specific type of capitalists because of the fact that they display a commercial orientation, follow a business strategy of economic diversification and do not directly apply capital to the production process in agriculture or industry itself, but gain control of the claims on the product of others through the outlay of merchant or financial capital. Closely linked up with these characteristics, South and Southeast Asian capitalists are termed a specific type of capitalists because they are dependent on government finance and protection, and on foreign capital and technology. Their profits are not based on production but are in essence rent incomes that are the result of distorted market mechanisms following a high level of state intervention and regulations. Capitalists in South and Southeast Asia are able to acquire a very large part of their income by making use of the difference between the market value of a government 'favour' and what the recipient pays to the government and/or privately to his benefactors in the state bureaucracy.

In his study on small-scale industrialists in Gujarat, Jan-Herre van der Veen emphasizes that the wide prevalence of a commercial orientation is the direct result of state intervention, more in particular of the import substitution strategy. Official efforts to ration inputs has created opportunities for entrepreneurs to earn windfall rents. It is the availability of these windfall rents that 'reinforces the *natural* tendency of small-scale industrial entrepreneurs to adopt a commercial orientation' (Van der Veen 1973: M-93). Similarly, Hein Streefkerk stresses that the most important explanation of the commercial behaviour of small-scale industrialists in India must be sought in both the economic structure and the social setting, which encourage rather than prevent diverse investments and the spreading of risks. 'Risk-spreading and inconsistency are obvious choices; commercialism is more rewarded than punished. Such an orientation will clearly be manifest by those with access to raw materials and sales markets and who exercise influence over politico-administrative matters' (Streefkerk 1985: 170).

In his study on Southeast Asia, Yoshihara Kunio identifies an inefficient superlayer of businessmen, whom he regards as either state-assisted or foreign capital-dependent capitalists. According to him, these businessmen are nothing more than front men-type capitalists who try to establish government connections for business advantage. They 'can be called rent-seekers because they are essentially seeking opportunities to become the recipients of the rent the government can confer by disposing of its resources, offering protection, or issuing authorization for certain types of activities it regulates' (Yoshihara 1988: 68). These capitalists are 'comprador capitalists' who depend on foreign technology and foreign capital and are not efficient enough to compete in an open international market economy (ibid.: 130-1). They are, in the words of James Clad, the region's 'duppies' (directly unproductive profit-seeking entrepreneurs) who are denounced as mythical business people practising rentier capitalism and thriving on facilities and favouritism, in which no real play of free market forces and free enterprise is admitted. They 'capture what economists call the 'scarcity premiums' that accrue to government-enforced advantages like monopolies,

9

quotas or licences. DUP means easy profit but little or no authentic production. It means economic activities that produce zero output while using up real resources' (Clad 1989: 16).

According to many authors, rent-seeking is excessive and pervasive in Southeast Asia today, and there are no indications that it will decline. Especially the Philippines, Malaysia and Indonesia are said to have a large number of rent-seekers who dominate the capitalist structure of these countries (Yoshihara 1988: 90). In the Philippines, they are known as 'crony capitalists', a term which was coined during martial law for those who benefited greatly from having close relations with President Marcos. Crony capitalists are private-sector businessmen who benefit enormously from close relations with the government. The habit of doing business favours for one's friends, may have reached state-of-the-art perfection during the Marcos years, but the expression describes equally well the type of commercial wheeling and dealing prevalent in many of Asia's other market economies (ibid.: 68).

In his study on the capitalist class in Indonesia, Richard Robison employs the term 'bureaucratic capitalist' for those Indonesian entrepreneurs who are connected to or dependent on state power.[7] Bureaucratic capitalists are those who once held or still hold bureaucratic posts, which they used for their initial capital accumulation; if they no longer hold bureaucratic posts, they still maintain close connections with the government and use these for their businesses. Robison emphasizes that to the extent that a group of indigenous capitalists has emerged in Indonesia, it is a bureaucratic bourgeoisie who is accumulating money without risks or entrepreneurship. For these bureaucratic capitalists, 'the use of politically secured economic privileges proved to be the path to capital accumulation rather than spontaneous transformation from a base of traditional small-scale trade and commodity production' (Robison 1986: 48). This does not only apply to the category of large, urban-based industrial entrepreneurs, but also to the rural elites, as indicated by the study of Frans Hüsken. He stresses that rural elites in Central Java were - and still are - ready partners in a coalition with the state, and they have benefited from it in many ways. 'Indonesian agricultural policy has focussed upon the local elites as the main agents of both political stability and economic growth by offering them new technologies, cheap credit, and an efficient marketing system. The present rise of a village elite ... is therefore to be attributed more to its position of *anak mas* (favourite child) of the state than to its entrepreneurial capacities as such' (Hüsken 1989: 327).

Along similar lines, Jomo uses the term 'statist capitalists' to characterize the dependent type of entrepreneurs who benefited from the New Economic Policy pursued by the Malaysian state since 1971. Under this policy, the development of Malay capitalism has been advanced by placing the onus of capital accumulation on the state. Statist capitalists are those entrepreneurs who are not involved in capital accumulation solely based on their own private property, but use the state apparatus to accumulate. They control capital accumulation by virtue of their access to state power and are popularly identified primarily with indigenous, Malay politicians, bureaucrats and businessmen. As a class, these statist capitalists have been ascendant since independence and dominant since the early 1970s (Jomo 1988: 268-72).

Studies that deal with the emergence of the capitalist class in South Asia place emphasis on the structure of the economy and on the aspect of economic diversification. Most scholars argue that a capitalist class did emerge but in a distorted way. The main distortion in their behaviour is their commercial orientation, the fact that they pursue a strategy of economic diversification instead of following one line of business. The specific nature of this distortion has to be explained by the type of government intervention and the social background of the entrepreneurs involved. Although there are differences in opinion as to the specific nature of the distortion - and hence the different terms employed to characterize the capitalist class - most scholars on South Asia agree that a class of capitalists did emerge in South Asia.

Studies that deal with the emergence of the capitalist class in Southeast Asia place more emphasis on the role of the state and on the aspect of dependency on rent incomes. Most scholars argue that it is the failure of emergence of an indigenous capitalist class that is one of the fundamental problems of these societies. The deep political and social divisions between Chinese and foreign capitalists on the one hand and indigenous capitalists on the other hand lie at the centre of these studies. It is the high level of state intervention in the economic sphere in order to counterbalance this Chinese and foreign dominance by supporting the rise of a class of indigenous capitalists that partly explains the emphasis on the aspects of rent and of dependency on state support, foreign capital and foreign technology. Although there are differences in opinion as to the specific nature of this dependency - and hence the different terms employed to characterize the class of capitalists - most scholars on Southeast Asia agree on the dependent nature of the capitalist class consisting of Chinese, foreign and to a more limited extent, indigenous capitalists.

11

Notwithstanding these differences in emphasis between those studies that focus on capitalists in South Asia and those studies that focus on capitalists in Southeast Asia, at the core of their conclusions often seems to lie a specific notion about the culture that underlies the economic behaviour of the Asian capitalists. The deformed nature of the capitalist class in Asia - its commercial orientation in South Asia and its dependency in Southeast Asia - is sometimes thought to be the direct or indirect result of the existence of a specific Asian mentality. Beneath the terms used to characterize the specific nature of the Asian capitalists lies the implication of a specific business culture, one in which public and private interests mix effortlessly. Despite local variations, it is this specific business culture that runs through the region. 'Doing business in the Asian archipelago usually depends, first, on personalities and, second, on patrimonial largess. Corporate label comes a poor third; expertise a dismal fourth. ... That underlying instinct - slicing off a cut of someone else's wealth rather than creating it yourself - runs very deep. ... The local economic élite appears to be willing to play a secondary role in the economy' (Clad 1989: 18 and 248).

According to this view, Asian capitalists have a strong inclination to be consumption-oriented, rather than production-oriented. They are not inclined to reinvest their profits in productive activities but are notorious for squandering their profits on luxury consumer goods and demonstrative expenditure on social ceremonies, all of which enables them to maintain a lifestyle of leisure and consumption. In their economic behaviour they have a preference for skimming off quick profits made by others, instead of acquiring profits on the basis of productive investments. In their economic and social contacts, they cling to family relations and ethnic networks. To a large extent their economic decisions are not based on rational criteria only, but are made with the purpose of enhancing their status within the community. In more general terms, it is usually 'thought that people in non-western societies are not prepared to make sacrifices now for the sake of future benefits. Behaviour directed toward the accumulation of goods or of capital is said to be lacking, the tendency being towards a way of life based on consumption. ... (This) consumption orientation signifies little interest in saving, which is outweighed by the desire for present gratification'.[8]

Following this line of reasoning, with its emphasis on a business culture characterized by commercialism and dependency, it is often argued that the specific pseudo- or non-genuine nature of the South and Southeast Asian capitalists results from the fact that most of the capitalists operating in India, Indonesia, the Philippines and Malaysia today have a mercantile background and are often traders by origin. There have already been doubts for a long time about the suitability of traders as industrialists. Many studies on Asia have emphasized that traders, given their stark profit motivation, cannot be considered a significant reservoir of industrial entrepreneurial recruits. They consider the production process as something fixed and static and are not prepared to invest more than the absolute minimum amount of capital in installations and machines. Ultimately, they remain committed to trade and quick turnover as the most important sources of profit. In all these respects, capitalists with a trading background are seen in contrast to true industrial entrepreneurs who are production-oriented, work within a long-term framework, are patient, tend to re-invest profits into industry, promote technological improvements, and are prepared to take risks.[9]

In sum, studies on South and Southeast Asia emphasize that socio-economic development in this part of Asia has been largely a constrained or deformed type of capitalist development. This conclusion is often based on references to the specific characteristics of the class of capitalists operating in these countries. More specifically, the existence of an autonomous, production-oriented class of industrial capitalists is mostly challenged by observers. The common view is that of a class of entrepreneurs who are commercially oriented and are heavily dependent on the government, foreign connections and biased regulations. Their behaviour and origin is generally thought to resemble that of the traditional dominant class of traders, who mobilize capital, organize labour and manage their enterprises along pre-capitalist lines of family and kinship. They are held to be notorious for dissipating their surpluses in conspicuous consumption and rarely make productive reinvestments of their profits but involve themselves, successively and simultaneously, in a wide range of disparate agricultural, commercial and industrial activities.

Because of these characteristics, capitalist entrepreneurs in South and Southeast Asia are thought to be a specific type of capitalist, indicated by the use of a specific terminology, such as 'commercially oriented capitalists', 'merchant capitalists', 'dependent capitalists', 'bureaucratic capitalists', 'comprador capitalists', 'statist-capitalists' and 'rent capitalists'. What all these terms have in common is disapproval of the economic and social behaviour of the present-day rich farmers, traders and industrialists in South and Southeast Asia[10]. More than a specific type of capitalist class, the class of capitalists in South and Southeast Asia is generally assumed to be a deformed, a pseudo- or non-genuine type of capitalist class.

13

3. 'Asian' Assumptions about the Early European Industrialists

Underlying this common view of the deformed nature of the capitalist class in South and Southeast Asia is the assumption that, either at present or in the past, either in Asia or in another part of the world, there did exist a class of pure, genuine and true capitalists. Without actually referring to the European path of industrial transition, it is this path and its emergence of a class of industrial capitalists that is frequently invoked as model or paradigm for the behaviour of the capitalists operating in South and Southeast Asia today. It is generally assumed that the early European industrialists, i.e. those entrepreneurs who operated in Europe at the time of the Industrial Revolution - mid-eighteenth to the mid/late-nineteenth century[11] - did meet the characteristics of true and genuine capitalists that the present-day South and Southeast Asian entrepreneurs are said to be lacking.

I name these assumptions about the early European industrialists that underlie studies on Asian societies, 'Asian' assumptions. By 'Asian' assumptions I mean assumptions that underlie Asian studies, more in particularly studies in which references are made to the class of Asian capitalists. 'Asian' therefore includes both the studies on Asia by Asian scholars and by non-Asian, mostly Western scholars.

The 'Asian' assumptions about the early European industrialists are not invented, but often have their origin in notions that can partly be traced back to debates among European historians about the nature of the Industrial Revolution in general and the emergence of the early European industrialists in particular. Central to the 'Asian' notion of the Industrial Revolution is the idea that this period in European history has to be characterized, first and foremost, as a radical and sudden transformation of society. In this view, the changes that took place in Europe between the mid-eighteenth and the mid/late-nineteenth centuries were sweeping changes which resulted in a break with the past in many aspects of economic life. The economic structure of Europe after the mid-eighteenth century was completely different from the period before. Two of the essential features of this radical and sudden transformation are generally thought to have been the emergence of a new production system, the factory, and the rise of a new producer, the industrialist.

The emergence of the factory-based production system followed the disappearance of the putting-out and domestic systems which had been the dominant forms of production during the period preceding the Industrial Revolution. The characteristic feature of the putting-out and domestic system was that production took place in small household establishments and domestic workshops. These systems of production were basically a combination of domestic work and commercial capitalism. At the top were rich men who were given various names by contemporaries but who are generally described by historians as 'merchant-manufacturers'. They either placed orders with master craftsmen in provincial towns, who then produced the desired goods in small-scale domestic workshops, or brought in the raw materials which they distributed to peasant-workers to process in their own cottages, often using simple machines (Wolf 1982: 270). The characteristic feature of the merchant-manufacturer was that he did not actively participate in the production process. He did not own the physical means of production; his capital was essentially circulating capital: raw materials, goods in the process of being manufactured and goods which had been sold but not yet paid for. Overall, fixed assets were only a very small fraction of industrial capital, and even in the few large-scale enterprises the ratio of fixed to circulating capital was low (Crouzet 1972a: 35). Basically, the merchant-manufacturer was a merchant, a trader, not an industrialist; he was an organizer of production and its financing, not a producer.

'The relationship of the merchant-manufacturer with the workpeople to whom he *gave employment* was ostensibly purely commercial, that of trader with customer or supplier: he sold them raw materials, he bought from them semi-finished or finished goods, and in the interval he granted them short-term credit (actually, he remained owner of the raw materials while they were being processed). ...

A merchant-manufacturer was a capitalist, who might own a large capital (tens of thousands of pounds sterling), but his was essentially circulating capital: stocks, work-in-progress, active debts. He did not own the physical means of production, which, with some exceptions such as knitting frames in the hosiery industry, remained the property of the workpeople; his fixed capital was only a tiny percentage of his total assets. ... Had we visited the warehouse of an ironmonger in the Midlands nail trade, no work other than storing, packing and delivering would have been observed. Everywhere most of the work was done in domestic workshops, which were the true basic units of production.

The merchant-manufacturer could participate in the process of production, mostly at the finishing stage; but, roughly speaking, he was not a producer, only an organizer of production and of its financing. Owing to the division of labour by process and to its atomization within the domestic system, a central organizing figure was essential to coordinate the endless movement of materials and of finished products and to be the link between *a vast army of small independent producers and multitude of dispersed customers*. In fact, although he frequently achieved a kind of vertical integration, one could say that the merchant-manufacturer organized production in its broad outlines but not in its details; he arranged the order and connection of the various technical processes but did not control them closely. ...

A large merchant-manufacturer could give out work to hundreds, even to thousands of people (there are examples in the mid eighteenth century); but he was not an industrialist' (Crouzet 1985: 5-6).

Many of these merchant-manufacturers did not confine themselves to one line of business. They were often polyvalent, with multifarious and widespread activities and investments. A number of them had interests in several industrial concerns at the same time. In addition to their chief interests, they were also involved in farming, cattle-fattening, mining, malting, property ownership, retail trade and pawnbroking. This behaviour could be observed among large as well as among small merchant-manufacturers, several of whom had their fingers in many pies. Many of them were not very specialized; they only worked part-time at their business and held a multi-minded devotion to their work. This plurality of interests of the merchant-manufacturers was partly dictated by prudence, by the need to spread risks, partly it resulted from the limitations which the state of technology and the market imposed upon the size of firms in many industries. Versatility of businessmen and absence of specialization in investment is therefore usually considered a trait which was normal at a time when functional specialization was little developed, but which became archaic with the advent of the Industrial Revolution (ibid.: 6-7).

From the mid-eighteenth century onwards, factory-based production is generally held to have become the dominant system of production in Britain. What was new about this factory-based system was the concentration of production in organizations under unified technical management and ownership, the employment of labourers and the widespread introduction of technological inventions, especially of power-driven machinery (Wolf 1982: 274). A vital component of the factory-based system was the increase in fixed capital at an unprecedented scale. From being commercial capital, a preponderant amount of capital became industrial, and from being floating and circulating capital, it became increasingly fixed capital, mainly as a result of the development of machinery, especially steam-power (Crouzet 1972a: 39). It is this dominance of the factory as the basic unit of production and the emergence, for the first time, of large concentrations of fixed industrial capital that are generally held to have been the essential characteristics of the Industrial Revolution.

The introduction of this new way of organizing production was established by a new type of businessman, the industrialist, who at the end of the eighteenth century was beginning to emerge in his own right and in growing numbers. This new businessman is generally considered to have contrasted the old type of merchant-manufacturer in many ways. Compared to the latter, production was at the centre of the industrialist's work, and not at its periphery. No doubt, merchanting skills, a sense of market opportunities and an ability to deal with commercial problems were as important for the industrialist as they had been for the merchant-manufacturer. In contrast to the merchant-manufacturer, however, the industrialist is thought to have intervened much more thoroughly and widely in organizing production. He was viewed as a 'practical man', often his own technical expert, as is shown in the following description of the pioneer civil engineer of the Industrial Revolution by William Fairbairn in 1861.

'The millwright of former days was to a great extent the sole representative of mechanical art ... he was an itinerant engineer and mechanic of high reputation. He could handle the axe, the hammer, and the plane with equal skill and precision; he could turn, bore, or forge with the ease and despatch of one brought up to these trades, and he could set out and cut in furrows of a millstone with an accuracy equal to or superior to that of the miller himself. Generally, he was a fair arithmetician, knew something of geometry, levelling and mensuration, and in some cases possessed a very competent knowledge of practical mathematics. He could ... draw in plan and section ... construct buildings, conduits, or water courses ... build bridges, cut canals ...'.[12]

It is emphasized that a distinguishing characteristic of this new type of businessman was that he 'fulfilled in one person the functions of capitalist, financier, works manager, merchant and salesman' (Wilson 1972: 381). Through the creation of the factory, industrialists achieved 'the concentration of ownership of workplace, means of work, source of power and raw material in one and the same hand' - their own.[13] As a result, a significant share of their capital was sunk into fixed assets. Instead of dealing largely in liquid resources, as was typical for the merchant-manufacturers, the industrialists are thought to have created very great elements of fixed capital and re-embodied them in the product over future time. They short-circuited and eventually eliminated the various intermediaries - especially the domestic small master and the merchant-manufacturer - who, under the domestic and putting-out system came between the labourer and the wholesale buyer of finished goods.[14] They organized production, brought together the capital and the labour force, selected the most appropriate site for operations, chose the particular technologies of production to be employed, devised new combinations of factors of production, were sometimes even innovators who initiated decisive economic change by breaking away from the constant trend towards equilibrium, bargained for raw materials and found outlets for the finished product.[15] In short, it is generally held that the industrialists that emerged during the Industrial Revolution were setting 'a new pattern of the complete businessman',[16] who gathered and merged a large number of roles in a single person.

Who were these new and complete businessmen, these first industrialists? Where did they come from and where did they acquire their capital to start their industrial enterprises?

Central to the 'Asian' notion of the early European industrialists is that these industrialists did not belong to the category of merchants or merchant-manufacturers. There are some indications that in the early eighteenth century, large traders who had earned money from the international trade had invested some capital in industry. 'The impression gained from the literary sources is that, in the west of England at least, the leading textile entrepreneurs were often exceedingly wealthy merchants' (Chapman 1973: 119). Central to the 'Asian' notion, however, is that such an extension of activity was not common among the European merchants, nor was it common among the merchant-manufacturers. On the whole, rich merchants and merchant-manufacturers in Europe are thought to have rarely invested the profits of their mercantile or putting-out ventures in industry; it was still more rare for them to be active partners in industrial firms. It is generally believed that those merchants and merchant-manufacturers who did own part of an industrial undertaking were merchants or merchant-manufacturers first and foremost, and their industrial activities were of only secondary importance to them (Crouzet 1985: 8 and 100).

This 'Asian' notion that the early industrialists in Europe did not originate from the ranks of the merchants or merchant-manufacturers follows Marx's description of the second road to capitalism, according to which a section of the existing merchant class began to 'take possession directly of production', thereby 'serving historically as a mode of transition', but becoming eventually 'an obstacle to a real capitalist mode of production and de-clin(ing) with the development of the latter.'[17] This view has been extended by Maurice Dobb who emphasizes that even though in the early days of the Industrial Revolution certain sections of merchant capital did turn towards industry and began to control production, at the most they might have prepared the way for capitalist industrialization, and may in a few cases have reached it, but they did not bring about any thorough transformation (Dobb 1976: 161). Dobb argued that a merchant-capitalist produced only as much as his trading business could accommodate, subordinating his productive activity to his interests as a trader. As a result, commercial capital continued to predominate over industrial capital. Being a merchant he had no interest in dismantling the various barriers and guild privileges in feudal society and in extending and broadening the market. On the contrary, he had every interest in maintaining the *status quo* of the society on which his profit rested. Because of the restrictive monopolies in the sphere of trade in which merchant capital was already entrenched, any considerable extension of the field of industrial investment would have remained limited, and the gains to be won by investment in industry, and hence the chance of a specifically industrial accumulation of capital, were likely to be modest, at least by contrast with the fortunes yielded by the carefully monopolized export trades (ibid.: 161).

Following this, the instigators of the Industrial Revolution in Europe are thought not to have originated from the traditional dominant classes of merchants and merchant-manufacturers but to have come from those social strata which had so far played a less prominent role in economic life: the class of independent self-sustaining yeoman farmers and small and middle-scale craftsmen. This notion is strongly based on Maurice Dobb's study in which he argues that it has been Marx's first road to capitalism which has been the dominant way in which the transition from feudalism to capitalism in Europe did take place.[18] According to this 'really revolutionary way', a section of the rural and urban producers themselves had accumulated capital and had taken to trade, and in course of time had begun to organize production on a capitalist basis, free from the handicraft restrictions of the guilds. Kulak yeoman farmers had started to purchase the labour power of their poorer neighbours, the cotters, to initiate the country cloth industry, and town craftsmen had begun to subordinate and to organize those very ranks from which they had recently risen. 'Socially, this was a class of *new* men, recruited from the lower segments of the provincial middle class. ... From this same stratum and milieu, too, came the *engineers* and *artificers* who designed, improved, and produced the new machines, along with water wheels, steam engines, and agricultural equipment' (Wolf 1982: 272). Being 'new' men who did not originate from the classes that dominated the old social structure, these new producer-capitalists had every interest in dismantling the various barriers and guild privileges that existed within the traditional domestic and putting-out system of production. It is from this social stratum of independent self-sustaining peasant-kulaks and small and middle-scale craftsmen that the early European industrialists are usually held to have originated.

> 'It is a familiar fact that ... the personnel which captained the new factory industry and took the initiative in its expansion was largely of humble origin, coming from the ranks of former master craftsmen or yeomen farmers with a small capital which they increased by going into partnership with more substantial merchants. They brought with them the rough vigour and the boundless ambition of the small rural bourgeoisie; and they were more inclined than those who had spent their time in the counting-house or the market to be aware of the detail of the production process, and so to be alive to the possibilities of the new technique and the successful handling of it. Among the new men were master clock-makers, hatters, shoemakers and weavers, as well as farmers and tradesmen. The yeoman farmer who had previously engaged in weaving as a by-employment had the modest good fortune to possess some capital and an acquaintance with industry and also land which he could mortgage or sell to raise additional funds. Many of the new names of the early nineteenth century were of this class' (Dobb 1976: 277-8).

This idea of the 'common' origin of the early European industrialists, as defended most prominently by Maurice Dobb, is closely connected to a more general belief that the chief agents of productivity in the early stage of European industrial development were mostly self-made men. This belief was widely prevalent in the nineteenth century. It is clearly shown in the writings of contemporaries such as Samuel Smiles, in his best-seller *Self-Help*, published in 1859, and P. Gaskell who maintained in his detailed account *Artisans and Machinery* (1836) that those 'who prospered were raised by their own efforts - commencing in a very humble way, generally from exercising some handicraft, as clock-making, hatting, etc. and pushing their advance by a series of unceasing exertions'. He added that 'many of the first successful manufacturers, both in town and country, were men who had their origin in the rank of mere operatives, or who sprang from the extinct class of yeomen' (quoted in Crouzet 1985: 40).

It is this belief of the 'self-made man' who sprang from a 'humble origin' of peasant-kulaks and craftsmen which has strongly influenced the 'Asian' notion of the early European industrialists. Following this view, the early European industrialists are held to have been independent businessmen. Whatever profits they accrued was due to their own hard work. There was no government assistance; all of them had to survive in an open, free-market economy with fierce competition. 'Born *in humble circumstances* (this is a standard expression), i.e. from modest or even poor families, they had started life as wage-earners, often working with their own hands; but, thanks to hard work, thrift, mechanical ingenuity and character, they had been able to set up their own business, to develop it and eventually to become wealthy and powerful' (Crouzet 1985: 37).

For their financial requirement these early European entrepreneurs are generally held to have operated independent of banks and other financial institutions. Most of the initial capital for their industries 'did not come from institutional sources,'[19] but was largely local, raised through connections of kinship, marriage, friendship, and local acquaintance. With hardly any institutional credit available, each industrialist had to find his own capital from existing personal or family accumulations (Kemp 1985: 20).

Viewing the 'humble' origin of the first industrialists and the fact that introduction of the factory system is thought to have required large concentrations of fixed capital, it is therefore generally assumed that 'capital had been a serious problem during the industrial revolution, and that innovators and entrepreneurs had been hampered by its scarcity' (Crouzet 1972a: 4). However, 'of serious shortage of capital we hear strangely little' (Wilson 1972: 391-2). Presumably business started from savings from the industrialist himself and grew by the assiduous plough-back of profits (Campbell and Wilson 1975: 15). And indeed, 'it has often been said that the early industrialists ploughed back their profits into their business' (Heaton 1972: 419).

This way of financing industry through the ploughing back of profits was possible because of the hard frugality and unremitting thrift these industrialists are said to have widely practised as part of an overall sober lifestyle. 'Their origins were often humble, and they were as hard on themselves as they were on others; business was their consuming interest and they continued to lead the simple lives to which they had been early accustomed, practising a stringent personal economy and a rigid austerity, which maximized their savings. They withdrew from their business each year only a small part of its profits for their personal needs, or else they paid themselves a small salary, hardly any higher than a skilled workman's wage' (Crouzet 1972b: 188). This practice of taking but a small part of the profits for their personal needs and leaving the remainder to accumulate in the business led to constant reinvestment and to a rapid growth of capital.[20] Establishing and expanding an industrial enterprise by saving from income has frequently been regarded as the only form that accumulation can take, or at least the only form it did take during the Industrial Revolution (Dobb 1976: 179).

This frugal living and thrifty behaviour of the first industrialists is considered to be the result of a pattern of deferred gratification, which may be defined as '... readiness to forgo present gratification in order to attain greater gratification of the same or another need at a later date' (Breman 1969: 15). It is this postponement of immediate gratification in the expectation of increased future benefits which is generally held to have been a guiding principle among the early industrialists in Europe. This method of industrial expansion through saving and reinvestment, although in the first instance imposed by necessity, is said to have quickly acquired a virtue of its own in the minds of these early European industrial entrepreneurs (Kemp 1985: 20). In this, they followed the prevalent ethic among the bourgeoisie who are held to have valued hard work and condemned idleness, and who frowned on spendthrift behaviour and praised savings (Stearns 1975: 47).

However, frugality and saving as such did not automatically lead to increased production. The regular reproduction of capital by the early European industrialists, involving the continual investment and reinvestment of capital for the end of economic efficiency, is therefore usually not just associated with a specific saving and frugal behaviour, but with an overall outlook among the members of this class. Characteristic of this overall outlook, this ethic of a very specific kind is the continual accumulation of wealth for its own sake, rather than for the material rewards that it could serve to bring. According to Weber, it is this combination of a work drive and a sober way of life that is the essence of the spirit of modern capitalism. Those entrepreneurs who are associated with the development of rational capitalism in Europe are said to have been characterized in their behaviour by an integration of the impulse to accumulate with a positively frugal lifestyle. 'When the limitation of consumption is combined with this release of acquisitive activity, the inevitable practical result is obvious: accumulation of capital through ascetic compulsion to save' (Weber 1976: 172).

It is this capitalist spirit, this combination of a labour ethos and a sober way of life, which differentiated the group of first European industrialists from their predecessors: the merchant-manufacturers and putters-out. Until about the middle of the eighteenth century the life of a merchant-manufacturer or '... putter-out was ... very comfortable. ... The number of business hours was very moderate, perhaps five to six a day, sometimes considerably less. ... A long daily visit to the tavern, with often plenty to drink, and a congenial circle of friends, made life comfortable and leisurely. The form of organization was in every respect capitalistic. ... But it was traditionalistic business, if one considers the spirit which animated the entrepreneur. ... Now at some time this leisureliness was suddenly destroyed. ... The old leisurely and comfortable attitude toward life gave way to a hard frugality in which some participated and came to the top, because they did not wish to consume but to earn, while others who wished to keep on with the old ways were forced to curtail their consumption. And, what is most important in this connection, it was not generally in such cases a stream of new money invested in the industry which brought about this revolution ... but the new spirit, the spirit of modern capitalism, had set to work' (Weber 1976: 66-8).

It was Weber who considered the motivation underlying this spirit of capitalism to be of a religious nature: the protestant ethic, the desire to acquire property not for enjoyment but for augmentation in the service of God and as a sign of His blessing.[21] Although he emphasized that '... we have no intention whatever of maintaining such a foolish and doctrinaire thesis as that the spirit of capitalism ... could only have arisen as the result of certain effects of the Reformation, or even that capitalism as an economic system is a creation of the Reformation' (Weber 1976: 91), religion is often considered to have been of importance for stimulating the principle of deferred gratification among the early European industrialists during their initial phase of capital growth. 'The fact that many, nay the majority of eighteenth-century industrialists belonged to nonconformist sects definitely reinforced their tendency to abstinence, hard work and thrift, and helped to keep them faithful to their simple and frugal way of life, even when they had made a fortune ..., and to discourage them from conspicuous expenditure or aping the upper classes; thus religion was a factor in the rapid accumulation of capital' (Crouzet 1972b: 188-9).

It is this capitalist spirit which is usually associated with the category of early European industrialists. Even though it was part of an overall ethic among the bourgeoisie of that time, it is generally held to have been most prominently present among those who initiated the process of industrial growth in Europe. Within the class of early industrialists, the capitalist spirit is generally held to have been the way of life, the form of consciousness that was best suited to the categories of yeomen and small and middle industrialists, and was not to be found in the 'hunger for money' and 'greed for gain' mentality, common among the monopolist merchants and usurers dominating the period preceding the Industrial Revolution. 'In general, at the threshold of modern times, it was not only, and not even mainly, the capitalist entrepreneurs of the trading patriciate, but much rather the up and coming layers of the industrial middle class which were the vehicles of the attitude that we have here labeled *spirit of capitalism*'.[22] Not only are the peasant-kulaks and middle-scale craftsmen turned capitalists thought to have possessed the necessary organizational abilities, but they are also considered to have personified the pattern of deferred gratification (Breman 1969: 22).

In sum, the 'Asian' assumptions about the early European industrialists consist of the following characterizations. Industrial growth in Europe was set in motion by a specific type of industrialist who had a peasant-kulak/yeoman or craftsman/artisan background and a single-minded devotion to his business. For him it was not the process of circulation that was the decisive factor but it was the production process that was at the centre of his activity and concern. Instead of following a policy of diversification like the merchant-manufacturers had done in former times, the early industrialist pursued a strategy of capitalization with resolute consistency by focusing all his energy on developing and expanding his business. He had a strong work ethos and practised a stringent personal economy and a rigid austerity. He reinvested the results of his labour ethos and his sober way of life by expanding production and realising continuous technological improvements. His behaviour was identical with the pursuit of profit, and forever renewed profit, by means of continuous reinvestments of his surplus through expanding and improving production, all of this with no other purpose than to generate more surplus on an ever-expanding scale.

4. *The Early Industrialists in Europe*

To what extent is this characterization of the early European industrialists, on which the 'Asian' assumptions are based, a valid characterization? At the risk of stating the obvious, it is important to emphasize that a type of characterization as the one described above basically ignores the possibility of diversity. Findings of economic historical studies show, for example, that the characterization of the early European industrialists as described above does not give a true representation of the category of first industrialists in France, nor does it give a true representation of all the categories of early industrialists in Britain. Several economic historical studies on France point out that the first French industrialists - i.e. those operating between ca. 1815 and 1870 - have to be characterized as conservative and consumption-oriented industrialists who were more intent on enjoying their wealth, power and prestige, than in pushing up the production indices.[23] The French businessman has been considered to have been insufficiently enterprising, preferring security behind tariff walls and seeking support from the state rather than investing in modern techniques and pushing into new markets (Kemp 1985: 68).

The behaviour of the first industrialists in France is held to have been characterized by widespread conservatism and timidity. The French businessman was a fundamentally conservative man, with a firm distaste for the new and unknown. He was reluctant to buy machines or to expand his production. Above all, the French entrepreneur prized security; and a secure market meant one well protected from foreign inroads. For most of the period of the Industrial Revolution, 'French industry and commerce were protected by a series of impassable duties and prohibitions which for most businessmen came to represent as much a permanent element of the environment as the ground on which their factories stood' (Landes 1972: 400). Many of the first French industrialists seem to have been influenced by this existing environment and to have absorbed its prevailing ethos: 'they preferred, it is frequently argued, security to risk-taking, they clung too long to obsolete methods, they looked to the government to protect them from foreign competition and retired early to live on their *rentes*' (Kemp 1985: 62).

With rare exceptions, French enterprise was organized on a family basis, mainly restricting its clientele to an intimate circle of friends and relatives. The entrepreneur conceived of his business, whatever its nature, not as a mechanism for the production or distribution of goods, but as a kind of purgatory to be passed through in order to establish a family fortune. Following the inferior place the businessman held in the French social structure, many entrepreneurs made efforts to rise into the ranks of the superior group, either through adjusting the lifestyle of the family, through marriage or through acquiring a landed estate, which was considered to be the safest of investments and an important criterion of social status. For that purpose, the firm was then sold up and the proceeds used to buy landed property or to invest in the *rentes* (government securities). Whether made as a form of conspicuous consumption or for more serious reasons, such investments by French businessmen are held to have been a significant obstacle to industrialization and to have contributed to the *rentier* character assumed by French capitalism (Kemp 1985: 69; Landes 1972: 404-6).

Similarly, economic historical studies on Britain point to the entrepreneurial failings of the second- and third-generation industrialists in Britain who operated at the end of the nineteenth century.[24] They emphasize the waning of the entrepreneurial energies of the founders' descendents for whom the industrial enterprise ceased to be an end itself and increasingly became a means for earning money to support a luxurious lifestyle. Wealth amassed in industry, it is argued, was often divided among heirs who did not pursue an active business life but merged into the professional upper-middle class. This could have meant a fall-off in the quality of business leadership in the sense that it became less concerned with pushing forward to acquire a position than to maintain a position gained in the past. With the members of the family more actively pursuing their own interests outside industry, many of the industrial firms were gradually allowed to run down. This overall 'decline of the industrial spirit' in the later nineteenth century was caused, in part at least, by the fact that many of the industrial entrepreneurs were too busy becoming gentlemen, living and spending on a lavish scale (Coleman 1973: 97).

According to this view, the behaviour of the second and third generation of industrialists in Britain clearly contrasts the behaviour of those who were among the first to set up an industrial enterprise. 'The selfmade man of the early Industrial Revolution was typically dedicated to accumulation: he ploughed back a high proportion of profits into the firm, taking out comparatively little for his own consumption. His sons and grandsons were not necessarily under such a pressing urge to accumulate. Inheriting the business as a going concern and a source of income they were already men of wealth and standing, susceptible to various social pressures which tended to separate their personal identity from that of the firm. Hence the tendency in the second and third generation for members of business families to diversify their interests and begin to behave like, or merge with, the existing leisured class of landowners. In a sense the firm tends to be administered more like an estate and less exclusively as an instrument of profit-making and accumulation' (Kemp 1985: 174-5). Overall, the category of early industrialists operating in Britain at the end of the nineteenth century is often held to have been more focused on spending their wealth than on earning money through productive activities (ibid.: 175).

These views on the first industrialists in France and the second/third-generation industrialists in Britain do to a large extent give a stereotyped picture of their behaviour. Economic history with regard to the Industrial Revolution in France and with regard to the late-nineteenth-century industrialization in Britain has gone through a process of renewal and reappraisal. Many authors have criticized the retardation or stagnationist thesis and have pointed at the unreliability of the unflattering portrait of the first French industrialists and the second/third-generation industrialists in Britain, to which numerous significant exceptions can be found.[25] Here it suffices to emphasize that these views, despite their stereotyped nature, point to the possibility of diversity among the early European industrialists. They indicate that the 'Asian' assumptions about the early European industrialists have to be questioned for at least these two categories of early industrialists in Western Europe, one of them operating in Britain, the country that was the first in the world to industrialize.[26] Following this, the test case of the 'Asian' assumptions about the early European industrialists seems to be the first industrialists in Britain, operating between the mid-eighteenth and mid-nineteenth centuries. These industrialists belonged to the very first industrialists in the world and are therefore considered to be the classical case of the emergence of a class of industrial capitalists.[27]

Before I discuss the findings of various historical studies on these first industrialists operating in Britain at the time of the Industrial Revolution, it is important to emphasize that the field of study is characterized by a lack of detailed research at the factory level and of reliable quantitative data on the origin and nature of the industrial entrepreneurs. No doubt, numerous economic historical studies have shed light on many useful data about the various sources from which the pioneers of the Industrial Revolution had drawn their initial capital. Several of these studies have been assembled in one volume, *Capital Formation in the Industrial Revolution* by François Crouzet (1972c). However, most of these studies are limited to one particular location or region, and they often confine themselves to one particular sector of the industrial economy. Although as a whole, they might present us with a large amount of valuable information, the quite disparate nature and quality of the data on which these studies are based, has resulted in the persistency of the problematic scarcity of knowledge about the composition of industrial capital and its owners during the first phase of British industrialization. At the end of Crouzet's introduction to the volume on capital formation, in which he presents an extensive overview of the studies available on the subject, Crouzet therefore concludes that: 'This survey of some problems concerning capital formation during the industrial revolution has shown that many of them remain unsolved, largely because of the lack of detailed research at the grass roots level and of reliable quantitative data' (Crouzet 1972a: 64).

On top of this problem of data scarcity and unreliability of the data used, many studies turn out to be based on biased samples. In his overview of the literature on *British Entrepreneurship in the Nineteenth Century*, P.L. Payne (1974) emphasizes that many studies on the early industrialists in Britain are founded upon a biased sample, i.e. they do not provide details of a representative collection of businessmen, but only of those who are known to have been important or who were sufficiently successful to have created conditions favourable for untypical longevity; hence the survival of their archives. He stresses that this surviving sample of archives is unlikely to be representative, simply because the records of those firms which were wound up or liquidated have usually disappeared.[28] 'What of the regiments of the anonymous; of those who made their major contribution to improving some process of invention, or who participated in short-lived partnerships, leaving perhaps only an entry in the docket books in the High Court of Justice in Bankruptcy?' (Payne 1974: 24). According to Payne we are perhaps too eager to generalize from the records of those that did survive - and these records, it will be freely admitted, are few in number - forgetting that our inadequate sample is far from random. 'On the basis of this biased sample, the temptation has been almost irresistible not merely to reconstruct a composite *complete businessman*, possessing all, or nearly all, the virtues, but to extrapolate these qualities not only to the many hundreds whose concerns have been mentioned in the county histories and the accounts of the local clergy, but even to those whose names have never been recorded' (ibid.: 31).

There have been some attempts to solve the problem of availability of reliable and unbiased data on capital formation and the origin of the first

European industrialists. A pioneer and highly suggestive example of an attempt to build up a representative sample of entrepreneurs is the study by S.D. Chapman on fixed capital formation in the early cotton industry, published in two separate articles (1970 and 1973). His study is based primarily upon the numerous insurance valuations of textile mills in the registers of the Sun Fire Office and the Royal Exchange, which, in the second half of the eighteenth century, took the lion's share of this kind of insurance business. The valuation figures taken from the registers were extrapolated to arrive at an estimate of total fixed capital formation among the textile entrepreneurs around 1730-1750 and 1770-1815.[29] This study is unique in the sense that it is based on relatively unbiased samples of the first industrial concerns. These samples do not only include those firms that were successful, but also those that were wound up or liquidated within a relatively short time span after having been established. A limitation of this study, however, is that it is confined to one industrial sector only, the cotton industry, and to some regions only, the west of England, East Anglia and the Midlands, neglecting, due to the unavailability of data, the northern regions and Scotland (Chapman 1973: 116).

This problem of limitations in scope, sectorally and regionally, applies to most economic historical studies on the emergence of the first industrialists. Those studies that attempt to quantify the origins of the first industrial entrepreneurs in Britain have been carried out within a specific sector and/or region. Many of them are discussed in Crouzet's study *The First Industrialists; The Problem of Origin* (1985), in which he presents an extensive overview of previous work done on this subject. In this book, Crouzet emphasizes the relative paucity of research into the origins of British industrialists, especially of the paucity of quantitative studies dealing with large populations of industrialists covering a wider region. According to him, this type of study is needed in order to be able to reach some precise and valid ideas about the social and occupational background of the first industrialists in Britain.[30]

This relative sparsity of data has led Crouzet to his project 'of building up a *national* sample, covering the main industries, *except mining*, including people from all parts of the country [Britain], and dealing with individuals who were active between the mid eighteenth and the mid nineteenth centuries' (Crouzet 1985: 54). Based on a wide variety of documents and sources, published and unpublished, he built up two samples of over 200 and 300 persons respectively; one of 316 founders of large industrial undertakings and one of 226 fathers of founders of large industrial undertakings in Britain (ibid.: 54-6). These samples, however, are neither random nor stratified, which gives his study some element of bias, arbitrariness and subjectiveness with regard to selection.[31] In spite of this limitation, Crouzet's study provides us with a unique set of data on the background and behaviour of a large number of first industrialists, not only in various industrial sectors, but also in various parts of Britain.

These studies by Chapman and Crouzet do not alter the conclusion of sparsity of data and their biased nature with regard to the origin and behaviour of the first European industrialists. As a matter of fact, lack of systematic evidence from which conclusions can confidently be drawn has been the main problem of most research on this subject. As a result, the field has been left open to unwarranted hypotheses and to notions of which the validity is seldom questioned. This in itself should make us suspicious about the validity of the 'Asian' assumptions about the origins and behaviour of the early European industrialists, as presented in the previous section. This suspicion increases when we look more closely at the findings of the economic historical studies on each of the various aspects of the origin and behaviour of the first British industrialists. In this overview, I do not pretend to give the subject an exhaustive treatment but only focus on those aspects of the emergence of the first industrialists in Britain that are important in understanding the discussion on the nature of the capitalist class in South and Southeast Asia today.[32]

In contrast to the notion of the Industrial Revolution as a radical and sudden transformation of society, recent research and analysis support the view that industrialization in Britain was gradual during the classic industrial revolution period. With this, it 'has restored traditional perceptions of the First Industrial Revolution as a drawn-out process in which the accelerations of the late XVIIIth century remain visible but are scarcely *discontinuities* let alone *take offs*' (O'Brien 1986: 294). In fact, the very concept of an 'industrial revolution' is misleading. Gradual industrialization has been the norm, explosive growth the exception (Cameron 1985: 2-9).

According to Goodman and Honeyman, 'recent research has also questioned the previously dominant belief in a linear progression of organizational systems from urban putting-out to urban factory, which regards the survival of pre-industrial economic forms into the era of modern industrialization as exceptional, outmoded and ultimately exhaustible under the rule of industrial capitalism ... the pattern was complicated and there existed other paths to development. The putting-out system, for example, survived for far longer than is usually appreciated even within the most advanced industrial activities' (Goodman and Honeyman 1988: 208). This is in line with Maurice Dobb's statement that 'we frequently find the two systems mingled together even at the same stage of production. ... Sometimes, especially in the eighteenth century, we find a capitalist clothier simultaneously employing workers in their homes and workers assembled together in one place on looms that he had set up in a single workshop' (Dobb 1976: 144). Survival of the putting-out system not only contributed significantly to the growth of the industrial economy, but also, in organizational terms, proved to be a vital part of the industrial complex.[33] Far from constituting a relic of the past, putting-out in nineteenth-century Europe was a dynamic form which responded actively to the demands of the capitalist system (Goodman and Honeyman 1988: 208).

As a result, business organizations and procedures prevalent in the pre-industrial economy persisted into the industrial economy, where they coexisted with other forms. Although there was a tendency towards concentration of production in organizations under unified management and ownership, in the overwhelming majority of cases such establishments were very small affairs during the early period of the Industrial Revolution. Chapman for example indicates that although many of the first weavers and woolcombers in Norwich did have a separate building in which they carried on their manufacture, these forms of concentration of production were often no more than very small workshops that were situated on the family's own premises. 'The workshop was invariably built adjacent to the entrepreneur's house, sometimes at the side, but often in the yard at the back, and with larger manufacturers formed part of a complex which might include a warehouse, dyehouse, stable, workers' tenements and, in country districts, barns and cowhouses' (Chapman 1973: 123-4).

Recent insights into the history of technology of the eighteenth and nineteenth centuries challenge the view of rapid and universal technical change embodied in conventional notions of the Industrial Revolution. The substitution of machinery for labour, which is an essential feature of the Industrial Revolution concept, was an equally uneven and protracted process as was the introduction of the factory organization (Goodman and Honeyman 1988: 205-6). Many industries were not initially affected by new methods at all (Stearns 1975: 84). In the textile industry, for example, as observed by Wilson, 'the new machinery ... involved no principles that an intelligent merchant could not grasp'.[34] New technology and mechanization, as it emerges in modern research, was in fact less novel and diffused very slowly during the early period of the industrialization process (O'Brien 1986: 294).

It is equally unlikely that the early stages of industrialization required such a big heave in investment as has sometimes been supposed. Capital requirements by the factory entrepreneurs were similar to those of the existing merchant-manufacturers; a relatively small proportion of their capital needed to be laid out in fixed plant and machinery (Kemp 1985: 18-20). The speed of growth of fixed capital and the difference between the old and the new industrialisms has often been overestimated, as is demonstrated in Sidney Pollard's study on *Fixed Capital in the Industrial Revolution in Britain* (1964). At the beginning of the Industrial Revolution, the threshold of entry into factory production was relatively low, especially in the textile industry, where even the largest production units were small, the plant rudimentary and inexpensive; consequently the initial outlay involved in setting up a factory was modest. In circumstances such as these a large number of industrial enterprises of the second half of the eighteenth century were founded on a small initial capital (Crouzet 1972b: 164-5). Therefore, fixed capital was the lesser part only of industry's total capital during this early period of the Industrial Revolution.

Moreover, many of the first industrialists used various capital economizing devices to escape large outlays of fixed capital. 'The really costly items were buildings and power, but, up to the late 1790s, relatively few buildings were built, specifically for the cotton trade. A cotton factory was almost any old building which had been set up for some other purpose - corn mill, farm or dwelling-house, barn, warehouse, etc. - and converted into a jenny workshop or an Arkwright-type water-mill. The ease with which existing premises could be thus converted helped many cotton spinners to start business with a very modest initial capital. In addition, many of them just rented the building in which they operated - or even part of it, the room- or floor-letting system being very common. Machinery, and even steam engines (which, anyway, did not exist in large numbers) could also be rented, or bought second-hand. During the initial stages of the Industrial Revolution, the requirements of fixed capital were thus very modest and the threshold of entry into factory production quite low, especially in the textile industries, of which, for quite a while, cotton was the only one to be largely mechanized. As much of this investment was undertaken by established merchant houses, they found little difficulty in making the marginal shifts from working to fixed capital which were necessary for building and tooling the early factories' (Crouzet 1972a: 38). This is confirmed by Herbert Heaton, who in his study on *Financing the Industrial Revolution* pointed out that the initial capital requirements for eighteenth-century would-be factory masters were very modest, especially as far as fixed capital was concerned.

'... they need sink little capital in building or equipment. An old flour or fulling mill, or even an old barn, could be adapted to scribbling, slubbing, or spinning.

32

... But the man with little capital need not sink *any* of it in plant. He could rent space - a single room, a floor, or a whole mill; he could buy power from his landlord, and he might be able to rent the machinery as well. ... It should now be clear that fixed capital requirements need not be large' (Heaton 1972: 414-5).

According to Crouzet, it would therefore be 'misleading to see the industrialists of the late eighteenth and early nineteenth centuries as heroic, gigantic, Titanic, Protean and Promethean supermen. There is some romanticizing in writings about *captains of industry ... rulers and conquerors* and about the crushing burden of functions which they had to carry in their factories and the extraordinary difficulties and responsibilities which they had to face. Undoubtedly the pioneers of the Industrial Revolution included a number of individuals who were outstanding, not only as businessmen *sensu stricto*, but also through their intellectual gifts and their strength of character. On the other hand, as Robert Owen wrote, there were also, even among successful industrialists, many *plodding men of business, with little knowledge and limited ideas, except in their own immediate circle of occupation.* ... (D)oubts have been expressed concerning the magnitude of the difficulties and problems which confronted early industrialists. It has been pointed out that the men who introduced the new techniques and the new capital equipment enjoyed a situation with monopolistic elements in favourable demand conditions, so that cost details and management mistakes could safely be neglected'.[35]

Moreover, the nature of the growth pattern was often conservative, being frequently characterized by sheer multiplication of existing plants and processes producing a fairly limited range of related products. Many small industrialists during the mid-nineteenth century did not even want to grow because they wanted to remain independent entrepreneurs who could run their enterprises all by themselves. They were able to make comfortable profits, and were strengthened in their resolve not to increase the scale of their operation beyond the size which would have involved partially entrusting their businesses to managers recruited from outside the family circle. All this made possible the continued existence of numerous small, often weakly-financed family concerns, many of whom chose to specialize in the exploitation of only a limited portion of the full spectrum of demand for related products. According to P.L. Payne, only a handful of the major pioneers of the Industrial Revolution would therefore apparently qualify as innovating and genuine entrepreneurs, while the vast majority of businessmen appear to have been imitative (Payne 1974: 13-16 and 34-45).

Instability in production was a common phenomenon among the first industrialists in Britain. Mortality rates for these firms were high; getting started was relatively easy, but staying in business turned out to be much harder. Many bitter individual failures occurred, particularly during the early decades of the nineteenth century, when many new firms were established (Stearns 1975: 89). Also in the organization structure instability was common among these first industrialists. Many firms were partnerships, often small, family-linked partnerships. A characteristic feature of these partnerships was 'their rapid turnover, the frequent changes among their members; partnerships were unceasingly created, supplemented, terminated. Indeed, their death rate was high; many factories or works had a chequered history and changed hands at frequent intervals, while many industrialists moved from mill to mill - several times in some cases - during their career' (Crouzet 1985: 59).

Plurality of interests was common among the entrepreneurs of the Industrial Revolution. It has been pointed out that, especially in the eighteenth century, men of capital were frequently interested in several enterprises of different kinds. In his study on *Industrial Capital and Landed Investment*, E.L. Jones, for example, remarks that 'the economic interests of the truly affluent and most powerful in trade, industry, and land did overlap in England' (Jones 1974b: 161). Industrial and commercial wealth was invested in land, while landowning and commercial wealth flowed to mining and industry (Crouzet 1972a: 54-5). 'In prosperous days the building of mills for lease to one or more tenants was a profitable way of investing capital. Large landlords were especially active, but merchants, manufacturers, and others who had money to spare turned it into bricks, mortar, and machinery, and then sought tenants' (Heaton 1972: 414-5).

Many of the richer industrialists were so to speak *brasseurs d'affaires* - rich people who had their fingers in several different pies, who were involved at the same time in, say, trade, banking, landowning, mining and industry (Crouzet 1985: 63). This pattern of diversification of economic interests among the first industrialists was not restricted to the upper class among the industrialists as is shown by Chapman's study of a thousand textile entrepreneurs in Britain between 1730 and 1750. His analysis of the assets of these entrepreneurs shows that 19.7 per cent of them had interests in farming - barns, linhays, hovels, milkhouses, cowhouses, dairies, granaries, etc - 17.2 per cent had interests in drink trade and shopkeeping, while 41.7 per cent had interests in property - buying houses and real estate (Chapman 1973: 128, table 5.3).

The investment policy that lay behind this capital formation among the textile entrepreneurs was the need to spread their risks in order to protect themselves against economic fluctuations. Their various assets allowed

34

them to accumulate some wealth and to improve their social standing, while serving as hedges against downturns in the textile market. The demand for textiles, particularly for sale overseas, was notoriously erratic, and prudent entrepreneurs retained or built up an alternative source of income wherever possible, preparing themselves for a quick shift of their resources if this proved necessary. As Chapman shows, the unwillingness of these industrialists to make a total commitment was often reflected in their insurance policies. Buildings, inns, and inn yards were easily converted into workshops and weavers' tenements, or mortgaged to obtain funds for investment.

'... it was a relatively easy matter to transfer capital from one industry to another within the region, not only because (as historians have known for a long time) entrepreneurs maintained a high proportion of their assets in liquid form, but also because their fixed capital investment avoided heavy commitment to any one industry. There was much less commitment to specific forms of capital like water mills than has been supposed, and buildings like workshops, dyehouses and barns were regularly transferred from one use to another. Entrepreneurs at all levels, from weavers and woolcombers to the merchant princes of the trade, were ready to invest in tenements and houses, and use them for various purposes, in pursuit of the same policy of diversification. The widespread practice of running two or three distinct businesses concurrently also reflects the same anxiety to avoid total commitment to the cloth trade or, for that matter, any other trade or manufacture. ...
The investment policy that lay behind this capital formation reflected some of the prime concerns of the entrepreneurs of the age: the need to limit their commitment to, and insulate themselves against, the erratic course of industrial change that had been characteristic of the economy as far back as anyone remembered or cared to record' (Chapman 1973: 136-7).

Following this brief description of the economic behaviour of these first industrialists in Britain, there is a common question which must be asked about these men: where did they come from and from where did they get their capital to start their industrial enterprise? Following Maurice Dobb's view, derived from Marx, that the really revolutionary transformation of production and the breaking of the control of merchant capital over production, was accomplished by men coming from the ranks of former craftsmen, some of the first industrialists were indeed craftsmen who had assumed the role of manager and owner of the means of production by investing their capital in the employment of other smaller craftsmen. As a result of the dramatic growth of the cotton industry, for example, cotton-spinners were the first large group of modern industrialists to emerge, and for a long time they were the most conspicuous and typical members of the new class (Crouzet 1985: 31). The class of artisans was also the breeding-ground for several famous machine-makers, including the greatest of them James Watt, who was an instrument-maker before becoming interested in steam-engines. On the whole, however, the rise among the craftsmen of a richer, capitalist element did not take place on a large scale. In his sample of 316 founders of large industrial undertakings and of 226 fathers of founders of large industrial undertakings in Britain between 1750 and 1850, Crouzet found that the group of independent craftsmen made up no more than five to eight per cent of these first industrialists.[36]

Although slightly higher, the working classes had in common with the class of artisans the fact that they supplied few industrialists. In Crouzet's samples they made up about ten percent of the first industrialists. He emphasizes that this is consistent with the figures put forward by other writers who indicate that 'very few first-generation entrepreneurs sprang from labouring groups - from the humblest levels of society without savings or schooling' (Crouzet 1985: 85). Engineering was an industry in which entry was always easy and opportunities for men with little capital, but with unusual skill and a gift for invention, were particularly good. It is not surprising, therefore, to find in this industry several industrialists who had started their career as manual workers, but from a few who made good (like Josiah Mason), they remained at best small masters for the rest of their life, and at worst they failed and went back to wage-employment. Several other industrialists of working-class origin could easily be cited, and the reality of a number of rags-to-riches stories cannot be disputed. However, quantitative studies invalidate the myth of the working-class self-made man - i.e. the idea that men from working-class families and/or former manual workers made up a majority or even a significant number of industrialists during the Industrial Revolution; they were only a small minority (ibid.: 89-94).

In an almost opposite direction, several economic historians have made attempts to rescue the landed aristocracy from the view that it took little part in the process of industrialization (Richards 1974: 414). They emphasize that landowners did play a noteworthy role in fostering industry. They were often instrumental in getting manufacturers started and contributed handsomely to the earlier industrial enterprises, next to being active in road- and canal-building, in mining, in transport and urban housing (Jones 1974a: 105-9). Their presence, however, was rather passive. They were often content to build (or to help to build) mills and to lease them out. If they owned blast-furnaces, forges and other establishments, they were either sleeping partners or tended to lease them to tenants rather than to operate them through salaried managers.[37] On top of that, as the eighteenth century progressed and industry became firmer on its feet, these landowners withdrew more and more from participation in non-agricultural ventures. Agriculture was a source of industrial entrepreneurs but it tended to be at a generation or so's remove.[38] 'After 1815 aristocratic capital was increasingly directed into securities, into stately homes, into conspicuous consumption, and most of all, into agriculture and land'.[39]

More than from the class of the landed aristocracy, it is argued that a substantial number of the first industrialists came from the ranks of wealthy farmers or small landowners - who described themselves as yeomen - and for whom farming is likely to have remained the main activity. Kriedte, Medick and Schlumbohm, for example, emphasize that 'wealthy, business-minded peasants and members of the village *bourgeoisie* often assumed a strategic function in the proto-industrialization process. They became the middlemen between domestic producers and the merchant. They constituted the personnel of the putting-out system's infrastructure. Occasionally, they became involved in the finishing of products, especially in bleaching if they had access to the necessary meadows. Often they, rather than the large putters-out in the cities, became the true agents of the industrialization process. They were closer to the production process and therefore more familiar with its requirements' (Kriedte, Medick and Schlumbohm 1981: 29).

This is only partly confirmed by the study of Crouzet who argues that 'it is true that some of these *peasant entrepreneurs* displayed unusual business ability and rose to become *small capitalists*, but they were far outdistanced by the true capitalists, i.e. the merchants and merchant-manufacturers, who made much larger fortunes' (Crouzet 1985: 21). Among the merchants, there was a clear disposition 'to extend their control over production and to assume some industrial functions (many cloth merchants took over dyeing and finishing, in their own workshops) - though this did not go very far. In several cases, it involved the mechanization and concentration in some central workshop of one or two processes, while most of the work continued to be done on a domestic basis' (ibid.: 28). Altogether, they made up about ten to fifteen per cent of Crouzet's samples, although he adds that studies of several other scholars indicate that their percentage must have been much higher; in some sectors the group of merchants made up between one-third to half of the number of industrialists (ibid.: 105). In Glasgow, for example, it was common during the second half of the eighteenth century for tobacco merchants to invest in the textile industry which developed in the city and its surroundings, and the richest of them had interests in several concerns at the same time.[40]

The initiative in industrial investment among the category of merchants did not come from the foreign trading companies. Initiative in this new direction lay not with the upper bourgeoisie concerned with the export market, but with the humbler provincial middle bourgeoisie, who was less privileged and less wealthy, but more broadly based (Dobb 1976: 193). In the case of cotton manufacture, for example, the entrepreneurs 'were not the big London merchants of Blackwell Hall, the London cloth mart, but rather the provincial merchants and their agents or factors involved in the commercial networks of the putting-out system' (Wolf 1982: 271-2).

The role of merchant-traders in the formation of the industrialist class is therefore certainly not as negligible as has often been maintained.[41] They are, however, clearly surpassed by businessmen who were already engaged in industry, i.e. by the group of manufacturers or merchant-manufacturers in domestic production, and owners and managers of already centralized establishments. In Crouzet's samples, about one-fifth of the industrialists were sons of persons already engaged in these kinds of industrial pursuits, while more than one-third of them were themselves already engaged in such an industrial pursuit at the time when they became industrialists (Crouzet 1985: tables 2 and 4) These figures fit in well with those of other writers (see e.g. Coleman 1973; Chapman 1973; and Goodman and Honeyman 1988). Moreover, many businessmen played the two roles of merchant-trader and merchant-manufacturer simultaneously.[42] By the end of the eighteenth century, for example, many merchant-manufacturers established spinning mills and/or calico-printing works, while continuing to put out work to domestic handloom weavers. During this same period, many merchants gained absolute control over production by becoming manufacturers themselves. As a result, merchants and manufacturers were often united in one person (Wilson 1972: 383). This dominance of the category of merchant-traders and merchant-manufacturers among the first industrialists in Britain proves, as argued by Crouzet, a kind of endogenesis:

'Industry bred a large number of the leaders who 'revolutionized' it. These 'insiders' came mostly from sectors of domestic industry which were identical with or closely linked to the branch in which they became factory masters; but they also originated in centralized establishments, sometimes in the same industry, sometimes in an ancillary activity, sometimes in a completely different branch. There were also 'lateral' moves, from an industry to a 'neighbouring' one which was more attractive and dynamic: a number of cotton-spinners had come from flax, wool and silk manufacturing. However, the main trend was towards integration, either forward or backward, more especially as one must take into account the merchants and traders who were closely linked with industry, because they either supplied it with raw materials or marketed its finished products' (Crouzet 1985: 116).

On the question of the sources of capital, i.e. the financing of industrial enterprises, both at their foundation and during their expansion, a large number of data have been collected by various scholars. The idea that many, if not most, industrialists were self-made men - which was a popular view during the nineteenth century - was exposed as a myth by twentieth century economic and social historians. The number of industrialists even in the Industrial Revolution who began without capital or connections of any kind was a minute fraction of the whole. 'Economic historians have not denied that, during that period, a number of self-made industrialists rose from poverty to great wealth, but they maintain that such spectacular successes were atypical and exceptional, while a large majority of industrialists came from rather well-to-do families, which could supply them with some capital to start in business and which also had useful networks of connections in their communities' (Crouzet 1985: 50-1).

Most firms were started with a small initial capital, which had been accumulated through pre-factory system manufacturing or merchant-manufacturing activities, or through the trading of industrial raw materials or finished articles. 'The landlords provided some [capital] by building mills. The merchants made a more important contribution; they supplied funds to some producers whose goods they were handling, or went into partnership' (Heaton 1972: 416-7). This also applied to merchant-manufacturers, whose capital appears as a very important factor in the birth of the factory industries. 'Naturally, these men, who were used to organizing and financing production and who provided *the historical transition*, as P. Mantoux wrote, *between the master-craftsman of the Middle Ages and the modern industrialist*, did not hesitate to encourage the rise of the factory system by investing in it the abundant capital at their disposal' (Crouzet 1972b: 170).

In many enterprises, capital from diverse sources was used. Small partnerships were common, they usually consisted of a group of relatives or friends, though sometimes a stranger was admitted as a sleeping partner (Payne 1974: 18-19; Heaton 1972: 416-7). Small artisan entrepreneurs for example often obtained outside help in order to found large factories. 'Of course we can find some which were founded solely on *artisan* or *commercial* capital, but generally speaking an entrepreneur had to rely on various sources to collect enough capital to found a sizeable new undertaking' (Crouzet 1972b: 183).

It is thus obvious that the founders of factory industries obtained capital from diverse sources, but that these sources were of unequal importance;

39

industry itself supplied most of the capital for its own transformation, while commerce provided an important supplementary reservoir. The part played by bank capital seems to have been very small (Crouzet 1972b: 182-3). Institutional sources hardly played a role in the supply of capital. Both private bankers and their joint stock descendants were commercial bankers, not investment houses (Heaton 1972: 416-7).

Overall, however, external supplies of capital were 'less important than the personal or family funds which the industrialists scraped together and ventured in the new productive equipment. The power of heredity and the vitality of the family as an economic group stand out whenever we examine the history of the pioneer manufacturers' (Heaton 1972: 416-7). Payne shows that 'although the firms that were limited were by far the most important in their spheres of activity, judged by size of unit and amount of fixed capital, the vast majority of the manufacturing firms of the country continued to be family businesses in the mid-1880s' (Payne 1974: 18-9). He even suggests that '... the over-representation of non-conformists among the *entrepreneurs who attained prominence* may be explicable not in terms of their religious precepts, their superior education or their need for achievement, but because they belonged to extended kinship families that gave them access to credit which permitted their firms, and their records, to survive, while others, less well connected, went to the wall' (ibid.: 26).

In order to expand, the pioneer 'firms usually borrowed - on mortgage, bond or note of hand - from family and friends, solicitors and attorneys (or through their agency), or from other manufacturers or merchants with whom they had connexions' (Crouzet 1972b: 191). Charles Wilson emphasizes that 'the parochial character of industry seems to me to go on much longer than is usually supposed: perhaps it still goes on. A knowledgeable businessman could write in 1903 as if the spread in industry of limited liability was a recent thing, and about the same time a soap maker could write to a Bristol rival: *personal knowledge of each other is a great factor in the cohesion of the soap trade*. ... He was only repeating what earlier makers had said: that *good fellowship* in the trade was worth ten shillings a ton' (Wilson 1972: 380).

Taken together, these economic historical studies point at the variety of the sources of capital which had been used for establishment, the resort by the first industrialists to the resources of their relatives and friends, on a personal basis, and the movement of capital between various branches of industry. In spite of all the external and family sources, it is often emphasized that what permitted the Industrial Revolution to proceed at a relatively swift pace was the fact that enterprises increased their capital by ploughing back immediately, regularly and almost automatically, the greater part, or even the whole, of their profits. Entrepreneurs who operated at the outset of the Industrial Revolution are said to have immediately reinvested most of their profits (and even the interest on capital) in order to finance expansion.

It is probably true that this state of affairs enabled a number of enterprises - possibly most of them - to finance expansion entirely from their own sources (Crouzet 1972b: 190-5). However, although there is every reason to believe that most of the additional capital required for expansion was indeed provided from the savings of the industrialists, this does not necessarily imply hard frugality and unremitting thrift as part of an overall sober lifestyle on the part of the industrialist's family. In the first industrial period, many industrialists indeed lived relatively simply: they lived close to their works, often in an adjacent house; the daily tour of the various departments was part of their life; they spent long hours at work, twelve or more a day, and closely supervised everything which went on in their factories. However, 'once they had built up their businesses and secured their fortunes, they nearly always relaxed somewhat, withdrawing more money and adopting a more comfortable way of life. Some of them bought landed estates and built themselves large mansions' (Crouzet 1972b: 189). We must therefore not over-emphasize the frugality of these early industrialists. They were conscious of the need to save money, for this was the source of investment funds, but they were also quickly open to new pleasures as consumers. 'During the factory-building years the visits to the cash box were restrained; but when the years of fixed capital investment were ended, different attitudes became apparent. ... The time had come for him to enjoy a more abundant life' (Heaton 1972: 421). They were eager to acquire a new standard of living and slowly began to separate themselves from the rest of the middle class. More and more successful business families sent their sons to public schools and many of them bought large mansions in which they employed servants and pursued a lifestyle of luxury and consumption. E.L. Jones, for example, remarks that 'much of the money which passed out of industry into land was squandered on prodigious bouts of port-drinking, on assemblies, race meetings, fox-hunts, pheasant battues. Resources were dissipated on unproductive activities like the gyrations of armies of flunkeys, the sonorities of private chapel building, the ordered informality of landscape gardening, the contrived futility of mock ruins and follies. A share of industrially created wealth constantly disappeared in these bonfires of good living for a small, landed class or was immobilized in their ornaments' (Jones 1974b: 179-81). One way in which their way of life is pictured is in the advertisements that offered for sale the mansions of those families that went bankrupt, as indicated by Heaton, who remarks that 'the bigger the firm the greater the noise when it fell and the longer the advertisement offering for sale its *delightful villa,* its *capital large dwelling house, pleasantly situated, with extensive plantations, pleasure grounds and gardens, trout stream, and picturesque views,* and its accumulation of *whatever is usually found in a well-furnished gentleman's house of the first respectability'* (Heaton 1972: 418).

During the first phase of European industrialization, the 'status of many families which produced industrialists was rather low, and even when they had made fortunes, industrialists were heartily despised by the traditional ruling class for their low birth and bad manners, and for decades they remained beyond the pale of *gentle* society' (Crouzet 1985: 142). In England, social standing depended to a greater extent than elsewhere on the ownership of landed property (Habakkuk 1953: 15-6). The purchase of landed estates by the first industrialists was therefore part of a widespread emulation of aristocratic lifestyles by the wealthier sections of the entrepre-neurial class. 'The early industrialist was making his way of necessity in a predominantly agrarian society. This environment, it may be supposed, was likely to exert strong pressures on his investment behaviour by swaying his personal aspirations. With his factory in a rural setting, with the ultimate social reference group the great landowners, the successful industrialist had every incentive to assimilate to the existing status structure by buying a large block of land. He had perhaps attained his wealthy eminence by novel means and untraditional attitudes, but to fix his children in the social firmament, as to the manner born, he would have to play by the rules of established, landed society. Few families held out long against its leisured, bucolic delights' (Jones 1974b: 160-2).

New entrants came from many industries, sometimes acquiring land by marrying into the landed gentry and from time to time into the aristocracy, more often by straightforward purchase. It is evident from the terms of the settlements on marriages between aristocrats and bourgeois heiresses that considerable material gains were necessary to induce the great families to contract them (Habakkuk 1953: 18-9). Those industrialists who entered rural society through the purchase of land wanted to seal their new status with new heights of splendour in their residence, extensive landscaping in their park and projects of improvements on their farms. 'Land, however, earned them less than the growth industries. ... The price for the social advantages and long-run prospects of landownership was the acceptance of a cash profit 1 per cent or 1 per cent lower even than investment in the funds or mortgages, and several per cent less than direct investment in industry' (Jones 1974b: 180). There are innumerable instances of this outflow of capital from industrial undertakings into the financially less profitable business of landowning. Some industrialists 'were alleged to have become so enamoured of landed pleasures that they dissipated their fortunes in gambling, entertaining, and other forms of social display' (Jones 1974a: 105). Many other cases, however, illustrate the fine balance between entry into land and further investment in industry among the industrial leaders of that time. In his study of the purchase of a large estate by the family of Richard Arkwright - the inventor of the Arkwright water-mill - Jones remarks that 'a shrewd, decisive man, Arkwright was eager to insert himself, or rather his sons, into the higher reaches of landed society, but for him an estate had also to be a fair investment. Arkwright bargained less closely than he would seemingly have done in his industrial role, but far more narrowly than the established country gentleman' (Jones 1974b: 162-78).

These changes in the lifestyle of the members of the industrialists' families were not restricted to the males only, but affected the life of the women in these families as well. In his study on *Leisure in the Industrial Revolution*, Hugh Cunningham, for example, describes the lifestyle of the middle-class women in mid-nineteenth-century Britain in the following ideal form:

'The perfect lady of the mid-Victorian years removed not only from worldly concerns, but also from household ones, was a symbol of her husband's wealth and status. Conspicuous leisure and conspicuous consumption were a mark of status, their utility for purposes of reputability lying in the element of waste common to both - waste of time and effort, or waste of goods. Dress for women, therefore had to be both expensive and impractical for productive labour; designedly uncomfortable, it testified in a general way to woman's economic dependence on man, and specifically to the status of a particular man. These concerns with status led, as is well known (and was much deplored at the time), to late marriages, so that the husband, well set in his career, could keep his wife in the manner which she had been led to expect as daughter' (Cunningham 1980: 131).

Overall, consumption and leisure were quickly becoming part of the lifestyle of the new industrialists. In this, they followed a general pattern of changes in lifestyle by members of economically upward mobile classes in society, as described by Thorstein Veblen in his *Theory of the Leisure Class*. In this study on social climbing in late-nineteenth-century America, first published in 1899, Veblen emphasizes that 'in order to gain and to hold the esteem of men it is not sufficient merely to possess wealth or power. The wealth or power must be put in evidence, for esteem is awarded only on

evidence' (Veblen 1931: 36-7). He shows that in many instances, conspicuous abstention from labour therefore became the conventional mark of
superior pecuniary achievement and the conventional index of reputability;
and conversely, since application to productive labour is a mark of poverty
and subjection, it became inconsistent with a reputable standing in the
community. Habits of industry and thrift, therefore, were not uniformly
furthered by a prevailing pecuniary emulation. Conspicuous consumption
of valuable goods was also a means of reputability. This need of vicarious
leisure, or conspicuous consumption of service, was for example a dominant
incentive to the keeping of servants.[43]

The ultimate industrial consequences of this draining of capital are hard
to assess. The opportunity costs of land purchases were high and economic
growth could surely have come faster without them. However, the achievement of the growth industries of the late eighteenth and early nineteenth
centuries was to keep up capital formation despite the persuasive attractions
of the new lifestyle. While part of the fortunes made in industry did leak into
landownership and into a conspicuous lifestyle, from the common-sense
point of view it appears that since manufacturing did expand, the counter-
attractions of wealth and rural life may have retarded, but could not block
industrialization (Jones 1974a: 105-6; and 1974b: 179-81). Moreover, 'it
should be remembered that many industrial pioneers operated in what was
in some ways a uniquely favourable economic environment. They faced
a buoyant domestic market buttressed, particularly in cotton textiles, by a
flourishing overseas demand in the exploitation of which they enjoyed
monopolistic advantages' (Payne 1974: 30). This remark is not intended to
belittle the achievements of the entrepreneurs of the Industrial Revolution
but to emphasize the fact that continuous investments and reinvestments in
industry by these early industrialists very well coincided with an increase in
wealth and conspicuous consumption.

Moreover, social ambition provided an immensely powerful motor of
business activity at the time of the Industrial Revolution. The pursuit of
wealth was the pursuit of social status, not merely for oneself but for one's
family, and this often meant the acquisition of a landed estate or the purchase
or building of a great house. Coleman therefore argues that 'no more then
than today was the maximization of profits an end; it neither was, nor is
today, the only means employed. ... The ends are more intangible and varied:
profits are a path to prestige, power, status, personal satisfaction, adventures
made, purpose and achievements gained' (Coleman 1973: 95-6). He also
puts forward the hypothesis 'that because manufacturing business was not
seen as an occupation fit for gentlemen and because successful businessmen

regularly withdraw their children from the business world by sending them through the gentlemanly educational process, the field was continually being cleared for a succession of thrusting, ambitious [industrialists] .... If successful businessmen, before and during the Industrial Revolution, had not been so anxious to attain a life of rural gentility might there not have ensued a much more rigid, inflexible, and unadventurous course of business enterprise than in fact there was?' (ibid.: 110-1). In a similar line, P.L. Payne states that 'those who have argued that this pursuit of non-economic ends inevitably involved a haemorrhage of entrepreneurial talent as the nineteenth century progressed, should perhaps balance this against what might be called the demonstration effect of conspicuous consumption or social elevation on the new men crowding in to emulate those who had already succeeded. One cannot help believing that many new thrusting firms would not have come into existence, or small established companies grown, had not their founders or owners, or their socially ambitious wives, seen or been aware of the tangible results of commercial or industrial success. ... These manifestations of success served to encourage the others' (Payne 1974: 25-26).

The foregoing social and economic profile of the early industrial entrepreneurs clearly indicates that many of them were drawn from exactly the same class as before. The new industrial changes in late-eighteenth-century Britain were linked organically and personally with an older economic world at every stage (Wilson 1972: 379). Only to some extent was the industrialist, who emerged during the Industrial Revolution, a new man. Continuity rather than discontinuity was the rule. Many of the first industrialists in Britain originated from the traditional dominant class of traders and merchant-manufacturers, who followed a strategy of diversification of their economic and social interests along with expanding their industrial affairs. Guided by a short-time horizon, these industrialists often did not reinvest their profits in the same enterprise but were notoriously quick to spread their risk by investing in different types of economic activities, either simultaneously or successively. Mobilization of capital and organization of the work was often done along the traditional, pre-capitalist lines of family and kinship. Although many of the first industrialists in Britain followed a lifestyle of frugality and sobriety, for many others investments of capital in their economic undertakings coincided with a lifestyle of luxury and consumption.

5. Asian Studies and European History

It is generally assumed that the emergence of the capitalist class in South and Southeast Asia is a historically unique phenomenon and the factors leading to it are so specific that they cannot be compared with the rise of the early industrialists in Europe. Any comparison of current industrialization in South and Southeast Asia with the European path of industrial transition is often regarded as historical determinism and therefore rejected outright.[44] To a large extent, this is of course correct. History does not repeat itself mechanically. A nineteenth-century pattern of development could hardly be repeated in detail today. All processes of change have their own prerequisites, which will differ from country to country and from one time to another. That the emergence of a capitalist class in South and Southeast Asia would be an exact duplicate of the rise of the class of industrial capitalists in eighteenth- and nineteenth-century Europe is of course ridiculous and should indeed be rejected outright.

However, there is some danger in arguing that every comparison of the emergence of the capitalist class in South and Southeast Asia with the rise of the class of industrial capitalists in Europe is always to be regarded as historical determinism and therefore to be rejected under all circumstances. The terminology employed to characterize the class of present-day capitalists in South and Southeast Asia shows that this has not prevented comparisons with their European counterparts from taking place, but has 'forced' these comparisons to get below the surface and thereby to become unverifiable. As a result, most references to the pseudo- or non-genuine capitalist nature of the present-day South and Southeast Asian entrepreneurs are partly based on assumptions about the origins and nature of European industrialists of which the validity is seldom questioned. Viewing the persistency and value attached to these characterizations, it is important that these assumptions are made explicit and are tested on their tenability.[45]

Economic historical studies on the early European industrialists, as discussed in this essay, show that most of the 'Asian' assumptions about the European industrialists are not tenable, not even for the 'classical case' of the first industrialists in Britain. They point to the fact that, because of lack of detailed research at the factory level and because of lack of reliable quantitative data, little can be said with certainty about their origin and nature. This in itself already casts doubt on the validity of the 'Asian' assumptions about the early European industrialists. From the findings of the economic historical studies on different sections of the first industrialists in Britain, as they were presented in the foregoing section, it appears that these 'Asian' assumptions are based on a stereotyped model and present us with a distorted view of the emergence of the class of industrial capitalists in Europe.

These 'Asian' assumptions/myths about the emergence of the class of industrial capitalists in Europe have often been challenged and have been invalidated by European economic historians for some time already. In his study on *British Entrepreneurship in the Nineteenth Century*, published in 1974, P.L. Payne, for example, argues that the pioneer industrialists do not fully deserve the notion of high quality of entrepreneurial performance that is usually attached to them. Based on an overview of the studies available at that time, he questions the assumption that drive and dynamism was a characteristic feature of the British entrepreneurs of the Industrial Revolution. He argues that it is not so much the paucity of scholarly business histories that has inhibited such inquiries, 'but it is more likely that, overwhelmed by our knowledge of the economic transformation that did take place between, say, 1780 and 1830, there has been too ready an acceptance of the idea that the entrepreneurs, the chief instruments of change, must deserve their reputations for courage and adventurousness, progressive efficiency, organizational ability and grasp of commercial opportunity, combined with a capacity needed to exploit it. But do they? This is too large a theme for adequate treatment here, but recent studies do raise the suspicion that the eulogistic aura enveloping the pioneers has been somewhat obscuring, if only because it is becoming increasingly clear that earlier assessments of the entrepreneur - which have been implicit rather than explicit - have reflected a biased sample' (Payne 1974: 30-1).

It is a curious fact that studies which have given so many contributions to a revision of old myths regarding the history of South and Southeast Asia have seldom made use of new insights among the European economic historians to question their own view of the origins and nature of the class of European industrialists, on the image of which they have characterized the emergence of the present-day capitalist class in Asia as being of a deformed, pseudo- or non-genuine capitalist nature. The discussion on Boeke's concept of economic dualism shows that this is not a recent phenomenon. In a volume, which brought together several studies by Boeke and other Dutch scholars on the concept of dualism in theory and policy, published in 1961, the editors emphasize that several Dutch economists and sociologists had levelled criticism at Boeke's dualism by accusing him of working with outdated conceptions and an imaginary view of Western society as being homogeneous in nature and guided exclusively by the economic motive. They refer to an essay by Van Heek who, in 1947, questioned Boeke's assumption of the homogeneous structure of Western society, which according to Boeke was characteristic of society in the phase of high capitalism, in contrast to the dichotomy of dualistic societies. This was confirmed by two studies on factory and unskilled workers in the Netherlands which demonstrated with clarity how little homogeneous Western society actually was (Wertheim et al. 1961: 24-5). Although these two studies made no explicit reference to the question of dualistic economics, the editors of the volume emphasized that, according to them, 'it seemed worthwhile to point out that, if the picture arrived at by modern scholars is to be accepted in its general contours, Dutch society is far from homogeneous either in its constituent elements or in its total structure; rather, it displays a clear analogy with the dualistic structure which Boeke believed to be typical of *Eastern* countries' (ibid.: 26). In the discussion on Boeke's concept of economic dualism that has followed since, the question of the validity of Boeke's picture of Western society has never been challenged again by scholars studying Asian societies. It is only the relevance of Boeke's concept for the socio-economic structure of Asian societies that has been questioned and often severely criticized.[46]

The fact that scholars studying Asian society do not question their assumptions on Western society, but accept these notions as the true image, is therefore not simply a matter of ignorance, but more of a choice for ideology over knowledge, as argued by Heather Sutherland (1993).[47] She emphasizes that the common view of Asian 'economic backwardness' as being rooted in the failure of Asian societies to maintain the 'proper' distinctions between political and economic spheres is based on ideologically inclined misreadings of European history. Her conclusion that 'all too often, our ideas of the past are dominated by an idea of *progress*, derived from simplified myths about European industrialization and growth' could equally well apply to our ideas of the present: 'While recent research has modified our views of those sturdy entrepreneurs who set us happily upon the right path, the comforting folk-tales still lurk in our memories and influence our assumptions' (Sutherland 1993: 11).

It is this simplified image and lack of historical perspective regarding the roots of European capitalist development that has enabled scholars studying Asian society to conclude that South and Southeast Asian industrialization seems to merit a terminology specific to the region.[48] Based on an unchallenged, stereotyped impression of the behaviour of the early European industrialists, being characterized as true and genuine capitalists, it is relatively easy, but highly questionable, to argue that the present-day South and Southeast Asian industrialists are to be characterized as a class of deformed, pseudo- or non-genuine capitalists.

Notes

1. The research on which this essay is based has been made possible by a fellowship of the Royal Netherlands Academy of Arts and Sciences. Valuable suggestions and criticisms on an earlier draft of the essay were given by Jan Breman, P.W. Kleijn, Dick Kooiman, L. Noordegraaf, Hein Streefkerk, Heather Sutherland and Charles Tilly. Part of the argument expressed in the essay was inspired by a paper of Hans-Dieter Evers on the comparison of market expansion and political pluralism in Southeast Asia and Europe (Evers 1990).

2. Over the past decades the debate over the originally Marxian concept of the Asiatic mode of production has grown considerably (see for example Thorner 1966; Krader 1975; and Sawer 1977). For an extensive discussion and a useful bibliography of the literature on the Asiatic mode of production, see Van der Wee (1985). For an overview of the debate on Boeke's characterization of the Indonesian economy as a 'dual economy', see Wertheim et al. (1966). See Furnivall (1944) for his characterization of the Indonesian society under Dutch rule as a 'plural society'.

3. With regard to the colonial period the terms 'colonial mode of production' (Banaji 1972; Alavi 1975) and 'peripheral capitalism' (Alavi 1981) have been employed among others. For an extensive overview of the 'mode of production debate in India', see Thorner (1982).

4. Hüsken 1989: 326. In a more recent publication, however, Hüsken again questions the value of the term 'hesitant capitalists' (Hüsken forthcoming).

5. Harriss 1982: 294. Harriss quotes here from *Party Life*, Journal of the Communist Party of India, 7th August 1978.

6. In a recent publication, Streefkerk reappraises and questions his earlier conclusions (1993: 26-39). In the concluding section of the essay, I will briefly refer to his arguments.

7. The term 'bureaucratic capitalists' was originally coined by Wittfogel in relation to China to define those who 'are owners of capital who act as commercial or fiscal agents for an apparatus state, no matter whether they are members of the officialdom or functionaries of the dominant religion, or persons of wealth who are neither' (Wittfogel 1957: 256).

8. Breman 1969: p. 16-17. In his study, Breman criticizes this notion.

9. See for an overview of this discussion with regard to the Indian situation, Streefkerk (1985: 162-64) and Rutten (1992: 171-75; 1994: 23-38).

10. The irresistible urge to use a specific terminology to characterize the capitalists in South and Southeast Asia is also shown in an article by François Raillon (1991). In this article he presents a critical evaluation of some of the newly introduced concepts. After stating that it is not fair to regard Indonesian business people as ersatz or *kabir* capitalists, Raillon himself, however, also comes up with a new term, probably intending it to be hopeful despite the rather derogatory connotation. According to him, Indonesian businessmen are 'infant capitalists' who 'still tend to maintain a close, umbilical relationship with the government, while they demonstrate growing initiative and capital accumulation capability' (Raillon 1991: 92-93).

11. This period differs for the different countries in Europe. For Britain the Industrial Revolution is usually held to have taken place between the mid-eighteenth and mid nineteenth century. In other Western European countries, such as France and Germany, industrialization started later and the Industrial Revolution is usually held to have taken place between the late-eighteenth/early-nineteenth and the late-nineteenth century.

12. W. Fairbairn, *Treatise on Mills and Machines* (1861: v); quoted in Coleman 1973: 104.

13. S.D. Chapman and S. Chassagne, *European Textile Printers in the Eighteenth Century; A Study of Peel and Oberkampf* (London, 1981: 39); quoted in Crouzet 1985: 9.

14. Crouzet 1985: 9. Crouzet refers here to S.G. Checkland, *The Rise of Industrial Society in England, 1815-1885* (London, 1964: 103).

15. Payne 1974: 14. Payne refers here to M.W. Flinn, *Origins of the Industrial Revolution* (1966: 79).

16. P. Mantoux, *The Industrial Revolution in the Eighteenth Century; An Outline of the Beginnings of the Modern Factory System in England*, revised edition, translated by Marjorie Vernon (London 1928: 386); quoted in Crouzet 1985: 9.

17. K. Marx, *Capital*, Vol. III, pp. 388-96; quoted in Dobb 1976: 123.

18. Dobb's study on the transition from feudalism to capitalism has provoked varied reactions, many of which have been assembled in one volume by Hilton (1976). I will return to this discussion in the next section.

19. Wolf 1982: 272. Wolf quotes here Perkin, *The Origins of Modern English Society 1780-1880* (Toronto 1969: 80).

20. Crouzet 1972a: 3. Crouzet refers here to T.S. Ashton, *Iron and Steel in the Industrial Revolution* (Manchester, 1924), pp. 48, 156-61, 209-11.

21. Weber states that 'in conformity with the Old Testament and in analogy to the ethical valuation of good works, asceticism looked upon the pursuit of wealth as an end in itself as highly reprehensible; but the attainment of it as a fruit of

labour in a calling was a sign of God's blessing. And even more important: the religious valuation of restless, continuous, systematic work in a worldly calling, as the highest means to asceticism, and at the same time the surest and most evident proof of rebirth and genuine faith, must have been the most powerful conceivable lever for the expansion of that attitude toward life which we have here called the spirit of capitalism' (Weber 1976: 172).

22. Weber, *Gesammelte Aufsätze zur Religionssoziologie*, Vol. 1, Tübingen, 1920, p. 49 f.; and cf. *ibid*, p. 195.; quoted in Takahashi 1976: 89 f.

23. See for example the studies by Cameron (1958), Hoselitz (1968), Landes (1951 and 1972) and Kemp (1962).

24. See for example the studies by Kindleberger (1964), Aldcroft (1964) and Wiener (1982).

25. See for alternative viewpoints on the French industrialists, e.g. Roehl (1976) and Cameron and Freedeman (1983). For alternative viewpoints on the British industrialists at the end of the nineteenth century, see e.g. McCloskey (1970) and McCloskey and Sandberg (1971).

26. Another example would be the case of the first industrialists in the Netherlands. It has often been argued that the Netherlands was comparatively late to industrialize because of the conservative, mercantile mentality of its businessmen, who were more interested in investing their capital in foreign bonds and domestic government securities than in financing industrial undertakings (see e.g. van den Eerenbeemt 1977). This thesis has been criticized by others who argue that in so far as one can talk of the 'unproductive' use of capital by the Dutch businessmen at the end of the eighteenth century, this did not have a negative effect on the process of industrial growth nor was it the result of a specific mentality among the owners of capital; their behaviour should be seen as an entrepreneurial strategy of flexible adaptation to the changing economic circumstances at that time (see e.g. Klein 1977).

27. The Industrial Revolution in Britain was the first in a long line of similar processes in Europe and is therefore often taken as the classical case or model. Although today few economic historians are prepared to accept the idea of such a model and increasingly view 'the First Industrial Revolution as something of a special and less of paradigm case for the economic history of Europe' (O'Brien 1986: 297), it is on this British model, and the notions attached to it, that most studies on South and Southeast Asia base their conclusions about the deformed, pseudo- or non-genuine nature of the behaviour of its capitalist class.

28. In a similar line, Charlotte Erickson wrote of her own study on the industrialists in steel and hosiery from 1850 to 1950 that they only 'represent the proportion of the whole population which the historical sources enabled us to study', (*British Industrialists; Steel and Hosiery, 1850-1950*. Cambridge, 1959: 7; quoted in Crouzet 1985: 66).

29. Chapman 1973 and 1970. Chapman admits that insurance valuations have to be interpreted with some caution, but he asserts that they are realistic and 'approached a conservative estimate of what would now be recognized as net capital formation' (1970: 235).

30. Crouzet mentions that so far there have only been two comprehensive attempts to quantify the origins of entrepreneurs in British industry as a whole, both by American sociologists: Reinhard Bendix and Everett E. Hagen (Crouzet 1985: 52).

31. Crouzet deliberately excluded a large number of industrialists by restricting the sample to the founders of large undertakings - 'the meaning of *large* being liable to vary according to period and place; he must be the owner of a significant part of the firm's capital and he must be actively involved in its management' (Crouzet 1985: 1). This was done partly in order to give some homogeneity to the sample and to isolate the true pioneers of the Industrial Revolution, partly it resulted from the simple fact that, despite the important role played by small firms during the Industrial Revolution, information about the small industrialists who ran them is very scanty (ibid.: 56-57).

32. From early on, the tenability of the notions on which the 'Asian' assumptions about the early European industrialists are based, have been questioned. Some of the notions that were discussed in the previous section have been challenged right from the moment they were ventilated and the discussions that followed have turned into major debates. Max Weber's thesis on *The Protestant Ethic and the Spirit of Capitalism*, originally published as a two-part article in 1904-05, immediately provoked a critical debate, which some ninety years later, has still not simmered down. And Maurice Dobb's *Studies in the Development of Capitalism*, originally published in 1946, also gave rise to varied reactions which have become known as the debate on *The Transition from Feudalism to Capitalism* (Hilton ed. 1976).

33. Large workshops and factories themselves long operated with subcontracting and craft labour markets, which means that factory owners were not, in any strong sense, works managers; often they did not know how to produce their commodities, but knew how to sell them (see e.g. Hanagan 1980; Hudson 1986; and Granovetter and Tilly 1989).

34. Quoted in Coleman 1973: 103.

35. Crouzet 1985: 11-13. Crouzet quotes here P. Mantoux, *The Industrial Revolution in the Eighteenth Century; An Outline of the Beginning of the Modern Factory System in England* (London 1928: 113) and R. Owen, *The Life of Robert Owen by Himself* (London 1857/1920: 50).

36. Crouzet 1985: 112. It might have been the equation of qualitative significance with quantitative importance that has led to the notion that the rise among the richer sections of the craftsmen was the critically important process in the early industrial development in Western Europe. Dobb himself admits that

'the details of this process are far from clear, and there is little evidence that bears directly upon it' (Dobb 1976: 134). This made Paul Sweezy remark that 'in fact, so little evidence, even of an indirect character, seems to be available that one reviewer felt constrained to remark that *it would have been desirable to find more evidence for the view, derived from Marx, that the really revolutionary transformation of production and the breaking of the control of merchant capital over production, was accomplished by men coming from the ranks of former craftsmen*' (Sweezy 1976: 53-54).

37. Crouzet 1985: 68. In his study of the West Riding wool textile industry between 1750 and 1850, Hudson argues that probably the most important contribution of landed wealth to the underpinning and expansion of industry was the sale and mortgage of farms and fields to raise industrial capital. He therefore concludes that '(D)irect financial involvement of landowners in sectors other than mining and transport may well have been limited but the complex relationship between landholding and the evolution of rural industry had important financial consequences which are all too often underplayed or ignored by historians' (Hudson 1986: 104).

38. Jones 1974a: 102-5. In fact, the transition from the land to the factory was generally indirect, through some other occupation. It is striking that 22 per cent of the industrialists in Crouzet's sample were the sons of people with interests in farming and mining, while only very few individuals - about four per cent of the total - were involved in farming or mining when they became industrialists; and most of these were in mining rather than in agriculture (Crouzet 1985: 122).

39. Richards 1974: 429-30. In this study, Richards describes the case of the family of the marquis of Stafford in the West Midlands, whose family after about 1820, in common with many of their class, increasingly demonstrated symptoms of withdrawal from direct contact with industry and retreated into a rentier function. In a similar line, Crouzet refers to B. Hoselitz and M. Kolin who found that in South Wales local landowners controlled almost all ironworks up to the 1740s, but that they disappeared from the ranks of entrepreneurs after the 1760s, despite the rapid growth of the iron industry (Crouzet 1985: 73).

40. Crouzet 1985: 7 and 100. It has traditionally been believed that such investment in industry only took place because these merchants had to adapt to the loss of their import and re-export trade in tobacco which resulted from the American Revolution and from American independence. Crouzet emphasizes that recent work has indicated that well before 1776 tobacco merchants in Glasgow were accustomed 'to investing on a fairly large scale in the industries of the town and of west-central Scotland, their capital being dominant in several of these' (ibid.: 100).

41. See for example Hagen (1962) and of course the study by Dobb (1976).

42. Moreover, many of the firms were partnerships with frequent changes among their members, as I already indicated. Crouzet emphasizes that alliances of a young man's entrepreneurial talent with the wealth of well-established senior men were common during the Industrial Revolution. This raises difficulties for establishing the background of the industrialists, inasmuch as in some cases it is not easy to ascertain, among a group of partners, who is 'active' and who is 'sleeping': 'a man could be an active partner in one firm and a sleeping partner in another - which, moreover, could be in a different branch of industry. More than this, the social background of the managing partners was often lower than, or at least different from, that of their sleeping associates; in the firm of Newton, Chambers and Co., the active partners were professionals in the iron industry, the sleeping partners were merchants and traders. The managing partners were the true industrialists, and it could happen that eventually they bought out their more moneyed but less active partners and acquired sole ownership' (Crouzet 1985: 59).

43. Veblen 1931: 38-39; 62-65; and 73-76. Veblen emphasizes that in order to bring any given item or element under the head of conspicuous consumption or conspicuous waste 'it is not necessary that it should be recognised as waste in this sense by the person incurring the expenditure. It frequently happens that an element of the standard of living which set out with being primarily wasteful, ends with becoming, in the apprehension of the consumer, a necessary of life; and it may in this way become as indispensable as any other item of the consumer's habitual expenditure. ... It would be hazardous to assert that a useful purpose is ever absent from the utility of any article or of any service, however obviously its prime purpose and chief element is conspicuous waste; and it would be only less hazardous to assert of any primarily useful product that the element of waste is in no way concerned in its value, immediately or remotely' (ibid.: 99-101).

44. Christer Gunnarson suggests that the outright rejection of the European experience as an object of comparison for developments in Third World countries can partly be explained by the Marxist and Rostovian connotations such a comparison involves. On a general level, both the Rostovian and the Marxist theories on economic development argued that what the newly industrializing countries are doing is to follow the road shown by the Western developed countries. It was Karl Marx who stated that 'the industrially more developed countries present to the less developed countries a picture of the latters' future'. W. Rostow followed a similar type of generalization in his 'Non-Communist Manifesto' in which he presented his take-off model of industrialization and economic progress in different stages by making a generalization from one example, England, to claim validity for all forms of development in the past, at present and the future. By postulating that only one type of industrialization exists, i.e. the European type of industrialization, of which the Third World type is a mere repetition, the Marxian and Rostovian

models represented a serious type of misinterpretation and thereby gave comparative history a bad reputation (Gunnarsson 1985: 189).

45. In this essay I have not discussed the influence of colonialism on the emergence of the class of capitalists in South and Southeast Asia. Although the behaviour of the capitalist class in Asia today has to be viewed within the wider historical context of colonialism, the purpose of this essay was a much more limited one. As stated in the beginning, its aim was to show what light is shed by the study of the early European industrialists on the selected issue of characterizing the capitalist class in contemporary South and Southeast Asia.

46. In an article published in 1964 (reprinted in 1993), Wertheim takes this argument even one step further, by asking himself: 'To what extent should our account of what happened in the Western world be revised on the basis of more recent experiences in Asia?' (Wertheim 1993: 55).

47. In an introductory essay to a recent volume on *Southeast Asian Capitalists*, Ruth McVey extensively discusses the changes in perception and ideology among the scholars studying Southeast Asian entrepreneurship. She shows, for example, how the 'Confucian culture' argument was first used to suggest why the Chinese were unlikely to make good capitalists and then received its present role of explaining why capitalist development in East Asia has been such a success (McVey 1992: 9). The way in which ideological considerations play a directing and compelling part in the researcher's view on the emergence of the capitalist class in Asia is clearly shown by Hein Streefkerk's detailed account of the reasons why he had to change in 1991 his earlier opinion of 1971 on the commercial style of industrial entrepreneurship in South Gujarat, India: 'My initial theoretical preferences and methodology, together with the ideological climate in Amsterdam and the prevailing discussions over development and underdevelopment, excluded processes which occurred in South Gujarat in the last two decades. ... [My earlier] conclusion that ... [the commercial] style of entrepreneurship necessarily leads to uncertain and unstable industrial development needs further re-examination' (Streefkerk 1993: 37).

48. The 'deformed' nature of the Asian capitalists does not seem to apply to the capitalists operating in East Asia. This is remarkable because only very recently, East Asian capitalists were being accused of, and characterized as imitating, non-genuine entrepreneurs, in comparison to those operating in the West. This recent change in appreciation of the nature of East Asian entrepreneurship is probably more the result of increasing economic and political power of these countries - especially of Japan - than of changes in the behaviour of their entrepreneurs. I hope to deal with this subject more extensively in a follow-up study.

References

Alavi, H.
1975 India and the Colonial Mode of Production. *Economic and Political Weekly*, Vol. 10, Nos. 33, 34 and 35: 1235-62.
1981 Structure of Colonial Formations. *Economic and Political Weekly*, Vol. 16, Nos. 10, 11 and 12: 475-86.

Aldcroft, D.H.
1964 The Entrepreneur and the British Economy, 1870-1914. *Economic History Review*, 2nd series, Vol. 17, No. 1.

Banaji, J.
1972 For a Theory of Colonial Modes of Production. *Economic and Political Weekly*, Vol. 7, No. 52: 2498-2502.

Bhaduri, A.
1973 An Analysis of Semi-Feudalism in East India. *Frontier*, Vol. 6.

Bobek, H.
1962 The Main Stages in Socio-Economic Evolution from a Geographical Point of View. In Philip L. Wagner and Marvin W. Mikesell (eds), *Readings in Cultural Geography*. Chicago, pp. 218-47.

Braadbaart, O., and W. Wolters
1992 *Rural Investment Patterns and Rural Nonfarm Employment in West Java.* Bandung: Akatiga Foundation, Centre for Social Analysis, West Java Rural Nonfarm Sector Research Project.

Breman, J.
1969 Deferred Gratification, Entrepreneurial Behaviour and Economic Growth in Non-Western Societies. *Sociologia Neerlandica*, Vol. 5, No. 1: 15-34.

Cameron, R.C.
1958 Economic Growth and Stagnation in France. *Journal of Modern History*, Vol. 30, No. 1.
1985 A New View of European Industrialization. *Economic History Review*, Vol. 38, No. 1: 1-23.

Cameron, R., and C.E. Freedeman
1983 French Economic Growth: A Radical Revision. *Social Science History*, Vol. 7, No. 1.

Campbell, R.H. and Wilson, R.G.
1975   *Entrepreneurship in Britain, Seventeen Fifty to Nineteen Thirty-Nine.* Atlanta.

Chandra, N.K.
1974   Farm Efficiency under Semi-Feudalism: A Critique of Marginalist Theories and Some Marxist Formulations. *Economic and Political Weekly*, Vol. 9, Nos. 32, 33 and 34: 1309-31.

Chapman, S.D.
1970   Fixed Capital Formation in the British Cotton Manufacturing Industry, 1770-1815. *Economic History Review*, 2nd series, Vol. 23, No. 2: 235-56.
1973   Industrial Capital before the Industrial Revolution: An Analysis of the Assets of a Thousand Textile Entrepreneurs c. 1730-50. In N.B. Harte and K.G. Ponting (eds), *Textile History and Economic History: Essays in Honour of Miss Julia de Lacy Mann.* Manchester: Manchester University Press, pp. 113-37.

Clad, J.
1989   *Behind the Myth: Business, Money and Power in Southeast Asia.* London: Unwin Hyman.

Coleman, D.C.
1973   Gentlemen and Players. *Economic History Review*, 2nd series, Vol. 26, No. 1.: 92-116.

Cunningham, H.
1980   *Leisure in the Industrial Revolution, c. 1780-1880.* London: Croom Helm.

Crouzet, F.
1972a   Editor's Introduction: An Essay in Historiography. In F. Crouzet (ed.), *Capital Formation in the Industrial Revolution.* London: Methuen, pp. 1-69.
1972b   Fixed Capital in the Industrial Revolution in Britain. In F. Crouzet (ed.), *Capital Formation in the Industrial Revolution.* London: Methuen, pp. 162-222.
1972c   (ed.), *Capital Formation in the Industrial Revolution.* London: Methuen.
1985   *The First Industrialists: The Problem of Origins.* Cambridge: Cambridge University Press.

Dobb, M.
1976   *Studies in the Development of Capitalism.* New York: International Publishers. [First edition 1947; revised edition 1963.]

Eerenbeemt, H.F.J.M.
1977   Bedrijfskapitaal en Ondernemerschap in Nederland 1800-1850.
        In P. Geurts and F. Messing (eds), *Economische Ontwikkeling en Sociale Emancipatie, Deel II.* Den Haag, pp. 1-31.

Evers, H.D.
1990   *Market Expansion and Political Pluralism; Southeast Asia and Europe Compared.* Bielefeld: University of Bielefeld. Paper presented at the EIDOS-Winterschool, Trade, State and Ethnicity.

Fegan, B.
1981   *Rent-Capitalism in the Philippines.* Manila: University of the Philippines. The Philippines in the Third World Papers No.25.

Furnivall, J.S.
1944   *Netherlands India: A Study of Plural Economy.* Cambridge: Cambridge University Press.

Gerschenkron, A.
1970   *Europe in the Russian Mirror: Four Lectures in Economic History.* Cambridge: Cambridge University Press.

Goodman, J., and K. Honeyman
1988   *Gainful Pursuits: The Making of Industrial Europe, 1600-1914.* London: Edward Arnold.

Granovetter, M., and C. Tilly
1988   Inequality and Labor Processes. In Neil J. Smelser (ed.), *Handbook of Sociology.* Newbury Park, California: Sage.

Gunnarsson, C.
1985   Development Theory and Third World Industrialisation: A Comparison of Patterns of Industrialisation in 19th Century Europe and the Third World. *Journal of Contemporary Asia*, Vol. 15, No. 2: 183-206.

Habakkuk, H.J.
1953   England. In A. Goodwin (ed.), *The European Nobility in the Eighteenth Century: Studies of the Nobilities of the Major European States in the Pre-Reform Era.* London: Adam and Charles Black, pp. 1-21.

Hagen, E.E.
1962   *On the Theory of Social Change.* Illinois.

Hanagan, M.
1980   *The Logic of Solidarity: Artisans and Industrial Workers in Three French Towns, 1871-1914.* Urbana: University of Illinois Press.

Harriss, B.
1981   *Transitional Trade and Rural Development: The Nature and Role of Agricultural Trade in a South Indian District.* New Delhi: Vikas Publishing House.

Harriss, J.
1982   *Capitalism and Peasant Farming: Agrarian Structure and Ideology in Northern Tamil Nadu.* New Delhi: Oxford University Press.

Heaton, H.
1972 Financing the Industrial Revolution. In S. Lieberman (ed.), *Europe and the Industrial Revolution*. Cambridge, Masachusetts: Schenkman, pp. 413-24.

Hilton, R. (ed.)
1976 *The Transition from Feudalism to Capitalism*. London: NLB, Foundations of History Library.

Holmström, M.
1985 *Industry and Inequality: The Social Anthropology of Indian Labour*. Cambridge: Cambridge University Press.

Hoselitz, B.F.
1968 Unternehmertum und Kapitalbildung in Frankreich und England seit 1700. In W. Fischer (ed.), *Wirtschafts- und Sozialgeschichtliche Probleme der Frühen Industrialisierung*. Berlin: Colloquium Verlag, Einzelveröffentlichungen der Historischen Kommission zu Berlin Beim Friedrich-Meinecke-Institut der Freien Universität Berlin, Band 1, Publikationen zur Geschichte der Industrialisierung, pp. 285-338.

Hudson, P.
1986 *The Genesis of Industrial Capital: A Study of the West Riding Wool Textile Industry c. 1750-1850*. Cambridge: Cambridge University Press.

Hüsken, F.
1989 Cycles of Commercialisation and Accumulation in a Central Javanese Village. In Gillian Hart, Andrew Turton and Benjamin White (eds), *Agrarian Transformations: Local Processes and the State in Southeast Asia*. Berkeley: University of California Press, pp. 235-65.
forthc. *A Village in Java: Social Differentiation in a Peasant Community, 1850-1980*. Dordrecht: Foris Publications.

Jomo K.S.
1988 *A Question of Class: Capital, the State, and Uneven Development in Malaya*. New York: Monthly Review Press.

Jones, E.L.
1974a Agriculture and Economic Growth in England, 1650-1815: Economic Change. In E.L. Jones, *Agriculture and the Industrial Revolution*. Oxford: Basil Blackwell, pp. 85-127. [Originally published in *Journal of Economic History*, Vol. 25, 1965.]
1974b Industrial Capital and Landed Investment: The Arkwrights in Herefordshire, 1809-43. In E.L. Jones, *Agriculture and the Industrial Revolution*. Oxford: Basil Blackwell, pp. 160-83. [Originally published in E.L. Jones and G.E. Mingay (eds), *Land, Labour, and Population in the Industrial Revolution: Essays Presented to J.D. Chambers*. London: Edward Arnold, 1967.]

Kemp, T.
1962   Structural Factors in the Retardation of French Economic Growth. *Kylos*, Vol. 15.
1985   *Industrialization in Nineteenth-Century Europe*. London and New York: Longman. [First edition 1969]

Kindleberger
1964   *Economic Growth in France and Britain, 1851-1950*. Harvard University Press.

Klein, P.W.
1977   Kapitaal en Stagnatie tijdens het Hollandse Vroegkapitalisme. In P. Geurts and F. Messing (eds), *Economische Ontwikkeling en Sociale Emancipatie, Deel I*. Den Haag, pp. 166-84.

Krader, L.
1975   *The Asiatic Mode of Production: Sources, Development and Critique in the Writings of Karl Marx*. Assen: Van Gorcum.

Kriedte, P., Medick, H. and J. Schlumbohm
1981   *Industrialisation before Industrialisation: Rural Industry in the Genesis of Capitalism*. Cambridge: Cambridge University Press. [Originally published in German in 1977.]

Landes, D.S.
1951   French Business and the Businessman: A Social and Cultural Analysis. In E.M. Earle (ed.), *Modern France: Problems of the Third and Fourth Republics*. Princeton: Princeton University Press, pp. 334-53.
1972   French Entrepreneurship and Industrial Growth in the 19th Century. In S. Lieberman (ed.), *Europe and the Industrial Revolution*. Cambridge, Massachusetts: Schenkman, pp. 397-412.

Lin, S.G.
1980   Theory of a Dual Mode of Production in Post-Colonial India. *Economic and Political Weekly*, Vol. 15, No. 10: 516-29; No. 11: 565-73.

McCloskey, D.
1970   Did Victorian Britain fail? *Economic History Review*, Vol. 23, No. 3.

McCloskey, D., and L. Sandberg
1971   From Damnation to Redemption: Judgements on the Late Victorian Entrepreneur. *Explorations in Economic History*, Vol. 9.

McVey, R.
1992   The Materialization of the Southeast Asian Entrepreneur. In R. McVey (ed.) *Southeast Asian Capitalists*. Ithaca, NY: Cornell University, Southeast Asia Program, Studies on Southeast Asia.

O'Brien, P.K.
1986 Do We Have a Typology for the Study of European Industrialization in the XIXth Century? *Journal of European Economic History*, Vol. 15: 291-333.

Payne, P.L.
1974 *British Entrepreneurship in the Nineteenth Century*. London: The Macmillan Press, Studies in Economic History.

Pollard, S.
1964 Fixed Capital in the Industrial Revolution in Britain. *Journal of Economic History*, Vol. 24. [Reprinted in F. Crouzet (ed.), 1972, *Capital Formation in the Industrial Revolution*. London: Methuen, pp. 145-161.]

Raillon, F.
1991 How to Become a National Entrepreneur: The Rise of Indonesian Capitalists. *Archipel*, No. 41: 89-116.

Richards, E.
1974 The Industrial Face of a Great Estate: Trentham and Lillerhall, 1780-1860. *Economic History Review*, 2nd series, Vol. 27, No. 3: 414-30.

Robison, R.
1986 *Indonesia: The Rise of Capital*. Sydney: Allen & Unwin, Asian Studies Association of Australia, Southeast Asia Publication Series No.13.

Roehl, R.
1976 French Industrialization: A Reconsideration. *Explorations in Economic History*, Vol. 13, No. 3.

Rutten, M.
1992 Artisan or Merchant Industrialists?: Small-Scale Entrepreneurs in the Countryside of West India. *The Journal of Entrepreneurship*, Vol. 1, No. 2: 169-214.
1994 *Farms and Factories: Social Profile of Large Farmers and Rural Industrialists in West India*. Delhi: Oxford University Press.

Sau, R.
1975 Farm Efficiency under Semi-Feudalism: A Critique of Marginalist Theories and Some Marxist Formulations - A Comment. *Economic and Political Weekly*, Vol. 10, No. 13: 18-21.
1984 Development of Capitalism in India. *Economic and Political Weekly*, Vol. 19: PE 73-80.
1988 The Green Revolution and Industrial Growth in India: A Tale of Two Paradoxes and a Half. *Economic and Political Weekly*, Vol. 28, No. 16: 789-96.

Sawer, M.
1977 *Marxism and the Question of the Asiatic Mode of Production*. The Hague: Martinus Nijhoff.

Sen Gupta, N.
1977   Further on the Mode of Production in Agriculture. *Economic and Political Weekly*, Vol. 12, No. 26: 55-63.

Stearns, P.N.
1975   *European Society in Upheaval: Social History Since 1750*. New York: Macmillan. [First edition 1967.]

Streefkerk, H.
1985   *Industrial Transition in Rural India: Artisans, Traders and Tribals in South Gujarat*. Bombay: Sangam Books.
1993   *On the Production of Knowledge: Fieldwork in South Gujarat, 1971-1991*. Amsterdam: VU University Press, Comparative Asian Studies 11.

Sutherland, H.
1993   *Political Power and Economic Activity in the Malay World 1700-1940*. The Hague. Paper presented at the seminar 'Historical Dimension of Development, Change and Conflict in the South', 14 and 15 April.

Sweezy, P.
1976   A Critique. In R. Hilton (ed.), *The Transition from Feudalism to Capitalism*. London: NLB, pp. 33-56. [Originally published in *Science and Society*, Spring 1950.]

Takahashi, K.
1976   A Contribution to the Discussion. In R. Hilton (ed.), *The Transition from Feudalism to Capitalism*. London: NLB, pp. 68-97. [Originally published in *Science and Society*, Fall 1952.]

Thorner, A.
1982   Semi-Feudalism or Capitalism: Contemporary Debate on Classes and Modes of Production in India. *Economic and Political Weekly*, Vol. 17, No. 49, pp. 1961-68; No. 50, pp. 1993-99; and No. 51, pp. 2061-66.

Thorner, D.
1966   Marx on India and the Asiatic Mode of Production. *Contributions to Indian Sociology*, No. 9: 33-66.

Tilly, C.
1983   Flows of Capital and Forms of Industry in Europe, 1500-1900. *Theory and Society*, Vol. 12, No. 2: 123-42.

Upadhya, C.B.
1988   The Farmer-Capitalists of Coastal Andhra Pradesh. *Economic and Political Weekly*, Vol. 23, No. 27: 1376-82; No. 28: 1433-42.

Veblen, T.
1931   *The Theory of the Leisure Class: An Economic Study of Institutions*. New York. [First published in 1899.]

Veen, J.H. van der
1973   *Small Industries in India: The Case of Gujarat State*. Cornell University: Ph.D. thesis.
1976   Commercial Orientation of Industrial Entrepreneurs in India. *Economic and Political Weekly*, Vol. 11, No. 35: M91-M94.

Weber, M.
1976   *The Protestant Ethic and the Spirit of Capitalism*. London: George Allen & Unwin. [Originally published in Gesammelte Aufsätze zur Religionssoziologie, Tübingen, 1920-21.]
1978   The Origins of Industrial Capitalism in Europe. In W.G. Runciman (ed.), *Max Weber, Selections in Translation*, pp. 331-40. [Originally published in Gesammelte Aufsätze zur Religionssoziologie, Tübingen, 1920-21.]

Wee, M. van der
1985   *Aziatische Produktiewijze en Mughal India: Een Historische en Teoretische Kritiek*. University of Nijmegen: Ph.D. thesis.

Wertheim, W.F.
1964   *East-West Parallels: Sociological Approaches to Modern Asia*. The Hague: W. van Hoeve.
1993   *Comparative Essays on Asia and the West*. Amsterdam: VU University Press, Comparative Asian Studies 12.

Wertheim, W.F. et al. (eds)
1961   *Indonesian Economics: The Concept of Dualism in Theory and Policy*. The Hague: W. van Hoeve.

Wiener, M.J.
1982   *English Culture and the Decline of the Industrial Spirit, 1850-1980*. Cambridge: Cambridge University Press.

Wilson, C.
1972   The Entrepreneur in the Industrial Revolution in Britain. In S. Lieberman (ed.), *Europe and the Industrial Revolution*. Cambridge, Massachusetts: Schenkman, pp. 377-95.

Wittfogel, K.
1957   *Oriental Despotism: A Comparative Study of Total Power*. New Haven: Yale University Press.

Wolf, E.R.
1982   *Europe and the People without History*. Berkeley: University of California Press.

Yoshihara, K.
1988   *The Rise of Ersatz Capitalism in South-East Asia*. Quezon City: Metro Manila, Ateneo de Manila University Press.